WOMEN'S ISSUES

PREGNANCY DISCRIMINATION AND THE SUPREME COURT

A CLOSER LOOK AT *YOUNG V. UPS* AND RELATED CASES

WOMEN'S ISSUES

Additional books in this series can be found on Nova's website under the Series tab.

Additional e-books in this series can be found on Nova's website under the eBooks tab.

WOMEN'S ISSUES

PREGNANCY DISCRIMINATION AND THE SUPREME COURT

A CLOSER LOOK AT *YOUNG V. UPS* AND RELATED CASES

DALE PITTMAN
EDITOR

NOVINKA

New York

Library of Congress Cataloging-in-Publication Data

ISBN: 978-1-63485-489-4

Published by Nova Science Publishers, Inc. † New York

CONTENTS

PREFACE

In 2015, the Supreme Court issued a decision in *Young v. United Parcel Service*. In the case, a United Parcel Service (UPS) worker named Peggy Young challenged her employer's refusal to grant her a light-duty work assignment while she was pregnant, claiming that UPS's actions violated the Pregnancy Discrimination Act (PDA). In a highly anticipated ruling, the Justices fashioned a new test for determining when an employer's refusal to provide accommodations for a pregnant worker constitutes a violation of the PDA, and the Court sent the case back to the lower court for reconsideration in light of these new standards. This book begins with a discussion of the facts in the *Young* case, followed by an overview of the PDA. The book then provides an analysis of the *Young* case, its implications, and a potential legislative response. Furthermore, the book focuses on sex discrimination challenges based on: the equal protection guarantees of the Fourteenth and Fifth Amendments; the prohibition against employment discrimination contained in Title VII of the Civil Rights Act of 1964; and the prohibition against sex discrimination in education contained in Title IX of the Education Amendments of 1972.

In: Pregnancy Discrimination
Editor: Dale Pittman

ISBN: 978-1-63485-489-4

Chapter 1

THE PREGNANCY DISCRIMINATION ACT AND THE SUPREME COURT: A LEGAL ANALYSIS OF *YOUNG V. UNITED PARCEL SERVICE*[*]

Jody Feder

INTRODUCTION

In 2015, the Supreme Court issued a decision in *Young v. United Parcel Service*.[1] In the case, a United Parcel Service (UPS) worker named Peggy Young challenged her employer's refusal to grant her a light-duty work assignment while she was pregnant, claiming that UPS's actions violated the Pregnancy Discrimination Act (PDA).[2] In a highly anticipated ruling, the Justices fashioned a new test for determining when an employer's refusal to provide accommodations for a pregnant worker constitutes a violation of the PDA, and the Court sent the case back to the lower court for reconsideration in light of these new standards.

This report begins with a discussion of the facts in the *Young* case, followed by an overview of the PDA. The report then provides an analysis of the *Young* case, its implications, and a potential legislative response.

---

[*] This is an edited, reformatted and augmented version of a Congressional Research Service publication R44204, prepared for Members and Committees of Congress, dated September 25, 2015.

BACKGROUND

According to Young, when she became pregnant, her doctor instructed her to lift not more than 20 pounds during the first half of her pregnancy and 10 pounds thereafter.[3] However, UPS had a policy requiring drivers such as Young to have the ability to lift packages weighing up to 70 pounds. Furthermore, the collective bargaining agreement stipulated that employees who were disabled due to an on-the-job injury or who had lost their driving certifications were eligible for a temporary assignment if their disabilities prevented them from performing their normal work. In accordance with this provision, UPS offered light-duty work to employees injured on the job, but it refused to provide such an accommodation to Young on the grounds that her pregnancy did not constitute an on-the-job injury.[4]

Young sued, claiming that UPS's failure to accommodate pregnant employees while providing light-duty assignments to other workers violated the PDA. The U.S. Court of Appeals for the Fourth Circuit, however, ruled in favor of UPS, holding that the company's policy did not constitute unlawful pregnancy discrimination.[5] According to the court, the policy was neutral with respect to pregnancy because pregnant workers were treated the same as other similarly situated employees who had suffered off-the-job injuries. Young appealed the ruling, and the Supreme Court agreed to review the case.[6]

THE PREGNANCY DISCRIMINATION ACT

Originally enacted as an amendment to Title VII of the Civil Rights Act of 1964,[7] the PDA prohibits pregnancy discrimination in employment. The amendment was adopted in response to the Supreme Court's decision in *General Electric Co. v. Gilbert*, in which the Court ruled that an employer's practice of excluding pregnant employees from receiving benefits under its temporary disability plan did not constitute sex discrimination in violation of Title VII.[8] Congress subsequently overruled the Court's decision by enacting the PDA, which amended Title VII to clarify that the statute's prohibition on discrimination in employment "on the basis of sex" includes discrimination "because of or on the basis of pregnancy, childbirth, or related medical conditions."[9] In addition, under the statute, "women affected by pregnancy, childbirth, or related medical conditions shall be treated the same for all employment-related purposes ... as other persons not so affected but similar in their ability or inability to work."[10] As a result, employers are required to treat women affected by pregnancy or childbirth in the same way they treat other employees who are similarly situated. It was a dispute over how to interpret this latter provision that was at the crux of the *Young* case.

Prior to the Court's decision in *Young*, federal appellate court opinions interpreting this provision of the PDA generally reflected two important principles. First, the courts typically agreed that if a pregnant employee was temporarily unable to perform her job due to the pregnancy, her employer was required to treat her in the same way it treated other employees who were similarly situated.[11] Thus, an employer who provided accommodations for workers who are temporarily disabled after suffering an off-the-job injury was required to provide similar accommodations to temporarily disabled pregnant workers. Such treatment could include providing light-duty, alternative assignments, disability leave, or unpaid leave to pregnant employees if such accommodations were granted to other employees.

Second, the courts generally held that the PDA did not require employers to provide accommodations to pregnant employees unless such accommodations were also available to nonpregnant employees, reasoning that to do so would require employers to treat their pregnant employees more favorably than similarly situated non-pregnant employees.[12] As a result, pregnant employees who challenged policies restricting light-duty work to those injured on the job were unlikely to prevail if employers uniformly denied reassignments to all disabled workers who were not injured on the job. In contrast, the Equal Employment Opportunity Commission (EEOC) had taken the position that an employer's failure to accommodate a pregnant employee under such circumstances was a violation of the PDA.[13]

Meanwhile, it is important to note that pregnant workers may be eligible for protections or benefits offered by laws other than the PDA. Indeed, Young's original lawsuit also contained a claim based on the Americans with Disabilities Act (ADA).[14] Although pregnancy generally is not considered to be a disability under the ADA, certain impairments that a woman experiences as a result of pregnancy may qualify as a disability for purposes of the statute.[15] If a pregnant worker can demonstrate that she has such a disability,[16] her employer must provide reasonable accommodations to her limitations unless such accommodation would impose an undue hardship on the employer.[17] An appellate court, however, rejected Young's ADA claim, ruling that "there is no evidence that Young's pregnancy or attendant lifting limitation constituted a disability within the meaning of the ADA."[18] As discussed in more detail below, recent amendments to the ADA may make it easier for pregnant employees to establish such disability claims.

YOUNG V. UPS

As noted above, the dispute in *Young* centered on how to interpret the second clause of the PDA, which provides that pregnant workers must be treated the same "as other persons not so affected but similar in their ability or inability to work.... "[19] In her argument to the Court, Young contended that the PDA's second clause requires employers to accommodate workers disabled by pregnancy in the same way that they accommodate employees who are disabled in other ways but similar in their inability to work. In contrast, UPS argued that its policy did not violate the PDA because pregnant workers were treated the same as other workers who were disabled due to offthe-job injuries. In a 6-3 ruling, the Court rejected the argument of both parties.

According to the Court, Young's interpretation of the statute would grant pregnant workers a "most-favored nation status" that would require employers who provided one or two employees with an accommodation to provide the same accommodation to all pregnant employees, regardless of any other relevant criteria, such as the nature of the jobs in question.[20] The Court rejected this approach as contrary to congressional intent, noting that disparate treatment law allows employers to establish policies that may negatively affect protected employees, subject to certain conditions. The Court also refused to defer to EEOC guidance that echoed Young's position, noting that the agency had altered its interpretation after the Court granted review in the case.[21] Likewise, the Court disagreed with UPS's interpretation because it would render the PDA's second clause "superfluous" and would be contrary to the unambiguous intent expressed by Congress when it overturned the *Gilbert* decision.[22]

Instead, the Court relied on an alternative interpretation of the PDA that appears to strike a middle ground between the approaches advocated by Young and UPS. This analysis rested in part on a distinction between disparate treatment and disparate impact cases. The former require evidence of intentional discrimination, while the latter involve neutral employment practices that have a discriminatory effect. The fact that Young's claim was based on an allegation of disparate treatment was central to the Court's ruling, which ultimately turned on the somewhat technical application of rules regarding the burden of proof in disparate treatment cases.

In general, a party seeking to establish a disparate treatment claim may prove discrimination in one of two ways: (1) by producing direct evidence that an employer policy or practice is explicitly based on a protected category or (2) by using a burden-shifting framework to create an inference of discriminatory intent.[23] Originally established in the 1973 case of *McDonnell Douglas Corp. v. Green*,[24] the burden-shifting model involves three steps. First, a plaintiff must establish a prima facie case of discrimination. Second, an employer must articulate a legitimate, nondiscriminatory reason for the disparate treatment. Third, the plaintiff must prove that the employer's rationale is a pretext for discrimination.[25]

Adapting the *McDonnell Douglas* framework, the *Young* Court held that a pregnant worker who alleges a violation of the PDA's second clause when an employer denies her an accommodation must establish a prima facie case of discrimination by showing that she is a member of the protected class; that she sought an accommodation; that the employer denied the accommodation; and that the employer accommodated others similarly situated in their ability or inability to work.[26] At that point, the employer must show that it had a legitimate, nondiscriminatory reason for denying the accommodation, although the administrative convenience or expense of accommodating pregnant employees will not be deemed to be a legitimate excuse. Finally, the employee may rebut this claim by demonstrating that the employer's rationale is pretextual.[27]

Further, the Court ruled, an employee may reach a jury on the issue of pretext if she provides "sufficient evidence that the employer's policies impose a significant burden on pregnant workers, and that the employer's 'legitimate, nondiscriminatory' reasons are not sufficiently strong to justify the burden, but rather—when considered along with the burden imposed—give rise to an inference of intentional discrimination."[28] According to the Court, a pregnant employee can establish that a "significant burden" exists if she can demonstrate that an employer provides accommodations to a large percentage of non-pregnant workers but denies such accommodations to a large percentage of pregnant workers. Based on this reasoning, the Court vacated the lower court's judgment and remanded the case so that the court could determine "whether the nature of the employer's policy and the way in which it burdens pregnant women shows that the employer has engaged in intentional discrimination."[29] Although the Court did not rule on the merits of Young's claim, it did appear to indicate that she could meet her burden of proof by arguing that the "combined effects" of UPS's policies accommodating three separate categories of non-pregnant employees, while simultaneously refusing to accommodate the majority of pregnant employees, imposed a significant burden on the latter.[30]

Ultimately, the Court's ruling preserves the ability of pregnant workers to sue under the PDA when an employer refuses to accommodate pregnancy-related disabilities, but it does not require employers to automatically provide accommodations under all circumstances. However, the significance of the Court's decision may be limited by changes that were made to the ADA during the course of litigation. Specifically, under the ADA Amendments Act of 2008,[31] Congress clarified that the definition of disability includes physical or mental impairments that substantially limit an individual's ability to perform major life activities, such as lifting, standing, or bending. The EEOC subsequently issued guidance stating that "[t]he effects of an impairment lasting or expected to last fewer than six months can be substantially limiting within the meaning of this [Act]."[32] This interpretation appears likely to make it significantly easier for a pregnant employee subject to a temporary lifting restriction to establish a disability claim under the ADA in the future.

LEGISLATIVE RESPONSE

The *Young* decision appears to have prompted several Members of Congress to propose legislation clarifying the meaning of the PDA. The most prominent of these bills is the Pregnant Workers Fairness Act (PWFA),[33] although other bills have been introduced as well.[34]

Introduced prior to the Court's decision in *Young*, the PWFA was designed to end the debate over the meaning of the PDA by explicitly providing reasonable workplace accommodations for employees whose ability to perform their jobs is limited by pregnancy, childbirth, or a related medical condition. Specifically, the legislation would make it unlawful for an employer (1) to fail to make reasonable accommodations for such employees unless the employer can demonstrate that the accommodation will cause undue hardship; (2) to deny job opportunities to such job applicants or employees if the denial is due to the need to make reasonable accommodations; (3) to require such job applicants or employees to accept an accommodation; or (4) to require such employees to take leave if another reasonable accommodation can be provided. In addition, the bill would adopt the ADA's definitions of "reasonable accommodation" and "undue hardship" and would borrow much of its structure from Title VII, including the latter's remedies, procedures, and enforcement provisions.[35] Like Title VII, the PWFA would also prohibit retaliation against any employee who opposed practices made unlawful under the bill or who filed a complaint or otherwise took part in a proceeding relating to allegations of unlawful practices under the bill.

Given the new legal landscape that has emerged in the wake of the Court's ruling in *Young*, it is unclear whether legislation related to the PDA will advance in Congress.

End Notes

[1] 135 S. Ct. 1338 (2015).

[2] 42 U.S.C. §2000e(k).

[3] Young, 135 S. Ct. at 1344.

[4] Id.

[5] Young v. UPS, 784 F.3d 192 (4th Cir. 2013).

[6] Young v. UPS, 134 S. Ct. 2898 (2014).

[7] 42 U.S.C. §§2000e et seq. Title VII prohibits employment discrimination on the basis of race, color, sex, national origin, or religion.

[8] 429 U.S. 125 (1976). For more information on Supreme Court decisions involving the PDA, see CRS Report RL30253, Sex Discrimination and the United States Supreme Court: Developments in the Law, by Jody Feder.

[9] 42 U.S.C. §2000e(k). The statute does contain a narrow exception if an employer can establish that having a nonpregnant employee is a "bona fide occupational qualification that is reasonably necessary to the normal operation of that particular business or enterprise." 42 U.S.C. §2000e-2(e).

[10] 42 U.S.C. §2000e(k).

[11] See, e.g., Equal Emp't Opportunity Comm'n v. Horizon/CMS Healthcare Corp., 220 F.3d 1184 (10th Cir. 2000); Adams v. Nolan, 962 F.2d 791 (8th Cir. 1992). Courts have also ruled in favor of pregnant employees who can demonstrate that they are being treated differently than similarly situated employees in other contexts, such as the provision of disability or unpaid leave. See, e.g., Byrd v. Lakeshore Hosp., 30 F.3d 1380 (11th Cir. 1994).

[12] See, e.g., Serednyj v. Beverly Healthcare, LLC, 656 F.3d 540 (7th Cir. 2011); Spivey v. Beverly Enters., 196 F.3d 1309 (11th Cir. 1999); Urbano v. Continental Airlines, 138 F.3d 204 (5th Cir. 1998).

[13] U.S. Equal Employment Opportunity Commission, Enforcement Guidance: Pregnancy Discrimination and Related Issues, July 14, 2014. The EEOC subsequently updated its guidance in light of the Young decision. U.S. Equal Employment Opportunity Commission, Enforcement Guidance: Pregnancy Discrimination and Related Issues, June 25, 2015, http://www.eeoc.gov/laws/guidance/pregnancy_guidance.cfm#IC1.

[14] Young v. UPS, 784 F.3d 192 (4th Cir. 2013). The ADA is codified at 42 U.S.C. §§12101 et seq.

[15] The EEOC has explained that complications during pregnancy, such as "a pregnancy-related impairment that substantially limits a major life activity," may qualify a woman for protection under the ADA. See 29 C.F.R. §1630.2(h) App.

[16] Under the ADA, an individual is deemed to have a disability if she (1) has "a physical or mental impairment that substantially limits one or more major life activities;" (2) has "a record of such an impairment;" or (3) is "regarded as having such an impairment." 42 U.S.C. §12102(1). Major life activities include a wide variety of daily activities—including, for example, performing manual tasks, standing, lifting, etc.—and the operation of major bodily functions. 42 U.S.C. §12102(2).

[17] 42 U.S.C. §12112(b)(5)(A). The ADA states that reasonable accommodations may include ensuring that facilities used by employees are readily accessible to and able to be used by individuals with disabilities. 42 U.S.C. §12111(9)(A). The EEOC has published regulations that provide additional guidance regarding the purpose and type of accommodations that may be required. 29 C.F.R. §1630.2(o) App.

[18] Young v. UPS, 784 F.3d 192, 200 (4th Cir. 2013).

[19] 42 U.S.C. §2000e(k).

[20] Young v. UPS, 135 S. Ct. 1338, 1349 (2015).

[21] Id. at 1351-52.

[22] Id. at 1352-53.

[23] TWA v. Thurston, 469 U.S. 111, 121 (1985).

[24] 411 U.S. 792 (1973).

[25] Tex. Dep't of Cmty. Affairs v. Burdine, 450 U.S. 248, 252-53 (1981).

[26] Young, 135 S. Ct. at 1354.

[27] Id.

[28] Id.

[29] Id. at 1344.

[30] Id. at 1354-55.

[31] P.L. 110-325, §4(a). In addition, the amendments specified that "[t]he definition of disability in this Act shall be construed in favor of broad coverage of individuals under this Act, to the maximum extent permitted by the terms of this Act." Id.

[32] 29 C.F.R. §1630.2(j)(1)(ix) App.

[33] H.R. 2654/S. 1512 (114th Cong.).

[34] See, e.g., H.R. 2800/S. 1590 (114th Cong.).

[35] The PWFA also incorporates multiple provisions found in several other employment discrimination statutes. Collectively, these statutes prohibit the same types of employment discrimination as Title VII, but cover employees who are not protected under Title VII, including congressional employees under the Congressional Accountability Act, 2 U.S.C. §§1301 et seq., presidential employees under Chapter 5, Title 3 of the U.S. Code, and federal employees under the Government Employee Rights Act, 42 U.S.C. §2000e-16.

In: Pregnancy Discrimination
Editor: Dale Pittman

ISBN: 978-1-63485-489-4

Chapter 2

SEX DISCRIMINATION AND THE UNITED STATES SUPREME COURT: DEVELOPMENTS IN THE LAW*

Jody Feder

SUMMARY

In its sex discrimination decisions, the United States Supreme Court not only has defined the applicability of the equal protection guarantees of the Constitution and the nondiscriminatory policies of federal statutes, but also has rejected the use of gender stereotypes and has continued to recognize the discriminatory effect of gender hostility in the workplace and in schools. This report focuses on sex discrimination challenges based on: the equal protection guarantees of the Fourteenth and Fifth Amendments; the prohibition against employment discrimination contained in Title VII of the Civil Rights Act of 1964; and the prohibition against sex discrimination in education contained in Title IX of the Education Amendments of 1972. Although this report focuses on recent legal developments in each of these areas, this report also provides historical context by discussing selected landmark sex discrimination cases.

* This is an edited, reformatted and augmented version of a Congressional Research Service publication RL30253, prepared for Members and Committees of Congress, dated December 30, 2015.

Despite the fact that the Court's analysis of sex discrimination challenges under the Constitution differs from its analysis of sex discrimination under the two federal statutes discussed in this report, it is apparent that the Court is willing to refine its standards of review under both schemes to accommodate the novel claims presented by these cases. The Court's decisions in cases involving Title VII and Title IX are particularly noteworthy because they illustrate the Court's recognition of sexual harassment in both the workplace and the classroom.

During the 2015 term, the Court issued a ruling in a high-profile case involving a claim of pregnancy discrimination in employment. In *Young v. United Parcel Service*, an employee challenged her employer's refusal to grant her a light-duty work assignment while she was pregnant, claiming that the employer's actions violated the Pregnancy Discrimination Act (PDA), a federal law that prohibits pregnancy discrimination in employment. In a highly anticipated ruling, the Justices fashioned a new test for determining when an employer's refusal to provide accommodations for a pregnant worker constitutes a violation of the PDA, and the Court sent the case back to the lower court for reconsideration in light of these new standards.

In its sex discrimination decisions, the United States Supreme Court not only has defined the applicability of the equal protection guarantees of the Constitution and the nondiscriminatory policies of federal statutes, but also has rejected the use of gender stereotypes and has continued to recognize the discriminatory effect of gender hostility in the workplace and in schools. This report focuses on sex discrimination challenges based on the equal protection guarantees of the Fourteenth and Fifth Amendments;[1] the prohibition against employment discrimination contained in Title VII of the Civil Rights Act of 1964;[2] and the prohibition against sex discrimination in education contained in Title IX of the Education Amendments of 1972.[3] Although this report focuses on recent legal developments in each of these areas, this report also provides historical context by discussing selected landmark sex discrimination cases.

EQUAL PROTECTION CASES

Constitutional challenges that allege discrimination on the basis of sex are premised either on the equal protection guarantees of the Fourteenth Amendment or the equal protection component of the Fifth Amendment. To maintain an equal protection challenge, government action must be established; that is, it must be shown that the government, and not a private actor, has acted in a discriminatory manner. While the Fourteenth Amendment prohibits discriminatory conduct by the states, the Fifth Amendment forbids such action by the federal government.

The Fourteenth Amendment provides, in relevant part: "No state shall make or enforce any law which shall abridge the privileges or immunities of the citizens of the United States; nor shall any State deprive any person of life, liberty, or property, without due process of law; *nor deny to any person within its jurisdiction the equal protection of the laws*."[4]

Although the Fourteenth Amendment requires equal protection, it does not preclude the classification of individuals. The Court has noted that the Constitution does not require things which are "different in fact or opinion to be treated in law as though they were the same."[5] A classification will not offend the Constitution unless it is characterized by invidious discrimination.[6] The Court has adopted three levels of review to establish the presence of invidious discrimination:

1. Strict scrutiny. This most active form of judicial review has been applied where there is either a suspect classification, such as race, national origin, or alienage, or a burdening of a fundamental interest such as privacy or marriage. A classification will survive strict scrutiny if the government can show that it is necessary to achieving a compelling interest.7 Generally, statutory classifications subject to strict scrutiny are invalidated.
2. Intermediate scrutiny. This level of review is not as rigorous as strict scrutiny. A classification will survive intermediate scrutiny if it is substantially related to achieving an important government objective.8 Sex classifications are subject to intermediate scrutiny.
3. Rational basis review. This least active form of judicial review allows a classification to survive an equal protection challenge if the classification is rationally related to a legitimate government interest.9 This level of review is characterized by its deference to legislative judgment. Most economic regulations are subject to rational basis review.

The Court's adoption of intermediate scrutiny for sex classifications did not occur until 1976. In *Craig v. Boren*, the Court declared unconstitutional an Oklahoma statute that prohibited the sale of "nonintoxicating" 3.2% beer to males under the age of 21 and to females under the age of 18.[10] Females between the ages of 18 and 21, however, were allowed to purchase 3.2% beer. Although the Court agreed with the state's argument that the protection of public health and safety is an important government interest, it found that the gender classification employed by the statute was not substantially related to achieving that goal. The statistical evidence presented by the state to show that more 18 to 20-year-old males were arrested for drunk driving and that males between the ages of 17 and 21 were overrepresented among those injured in traffic accidents could not establish that the statute's gender classification was substantially related to ensuring public health and safety.

In establishing an intermediate level of review for sex classifications, the *Craig* Court identified what has been a common theme in sex discrimination cases under the Fourteenth Amendment: stereotypes and generalizations about the sexes.[11] In *Craig*, the Court acknowledged its previous invalidation of statutes that premised their classifications on misconceptions concerning the role of females. The Court's rejection of the use of stereotypes may be seen in many of the cases in this area.[12] The Court's more recent decisions similarly allude to the use of stereotypes and generalizations.

For example, in *J.E.B. v. Alabama*, the Court determined that the state could not use its peremptory challenges to exclude male jurors in a paternity and child support action.[13] In reaching its conclusion, the Court reviewed the historical exclusion of women from juries because of the belief that women were "too fragile and virginal to withstand the polluted courtroom atmosphere."[14] In *J.E.B.*, the Court questioned the state's generalizations of male jurors being more sympathetic to the arguments of a father in a paternity action and female jurors being more receptive to the mother. The Court maintained that state actors who exercise peremptory challenges in reliance on gender stereotypes "ratify and reinforce prejudicial views of the relative abilities of men and women."[15] The Court feared that this discriminatory use of peremptory challenges not only would raise questions about the fairness of the entire proceeding, but also would create the impression that the judicial system had acquiesced in the denial of participation by one gender.

In *U.S. v. Virginia*, the Court conducted a more searching form of intermediate scrutiny to find unconstitutional the exclusion of women from the Virginia Military Institute (VMI).[16] Although the Court reiterated that a classification must be substantially related to an important government interest, the Court also required the state to establish an "exceedingly persuasive justification" for its actions.[17]

Virginia advanced two arguments in support of VMI's exclusion of women: first, the single-sex education offered by VMI contributed to a diversity of educational approaches in Virginia; second, VMI employed a unique adversative method of training that would be destroyed if women were admitted.

After reviewing the history of Virginia's educational system, the Court concluded that VMI was not established or maintained to promote educational diversity. In fact, VMI's "historic and constant plan" was to offer a unique educational benefit to only men,[18] rather than to complement other Virginia institutions by providing a single-sex educational option. Further, the Court recognized Virginia's historic reluctance to allow women to pursue higher education. Any interest Virginia had in maintaining educational diversity seemed to be "proffered in response to litigation."[19]

In addressing Virginia's second argument, the Court expressed concern over the exclusion of women from VMI because of generalizations about their ability. While acknowledging that most women would probably not choose the adversative method, the Court maintained that some women had the will and capacity to succeed at VMI. Following *J.E.B.*, the Court cautioned state actors not to rely on overbroad generalizations to perpetuate patterns of discrimination. While the Court believed that the adversative method did promote important goals, it concluded that the exclusion of women was not substantially related to achieving those goals.

After determining that VMI's exclusion of women violated the Fourteenth Amendment, the Court reviewed the state's remedy, a separate program for women. Virginia established the Virginia Women's Institute for Leadership (VWIL) following the adverse decision of the court of appeals. Unlike VMI, VWIL did not use the adversative method because it was believed to be inappropriate for most women,[20] and VWIL lacked the faculty, facilities, and course offerings available at VMI. Because VWIL was not a comparable single-sex institution for women, the Court concluded that it was an inadequate remedy for the state's equal protection violations. VMI subsequently became coeducational.

The Court's most recent equal protection pronouncements with respect to sex discrimination both involved immigration issues. In *Miller v. Albright*, the Court considered a challenge to §309 of the Immigration and Nationality Act.[21] The petitioner, the child of an American father and a Filipino mother, contended that §309 imposed additional requirements for establishing American citizenship when a child is fathered by an American citizen outside of the United States.[22] For children born of a citizen mother and an alien father, citizenship is established at birth. However, for children born of a citizen father and an alien mother, citizenship is not established until the father or the child takes affirmative steps to confirm their relationship by the child's eighteenth birthday. In this case, the petitioner's father did not attempt to establish his relationship with his daughter until after her eighteenth birthday. Thus, the petitioner's application for citizenship was denied.

The case produced five different opinions. While six justices agreed that the petitioner's complaint should be dismissed, they provided different reasons for this conclusion. Justices Stevens and Rehnquist contended that the petitioner's complaint lacked merit, maintaining that §309's distinction between "illegitimate" children of U.S. citizen mothers and "illegitimate" children of U.S. citizen fathers is permissible under heightened scrutiny because it is "eminently reasonable and justified by important Government policies."[23] Justices O'Connor and Kennedy contended, however, that the distinction could withstand only rational basis review and should not satisfy the kind of heightened scrutiny Justice Stevens seemed to conduct. Setting aside the issue of §309's constitutionality, Justices O'Connor and Kennedy believed that the petitioner lacked the standing necessary to even pursue her claim. Finally, Justices Scalia and Thomas contended that the petitioner's complaint should be dismissed because the Court lacks the power to confer citizenship. Having acknowledged that Congress has the exclusive authority to grant citizenship, Justices Scalia and Thomas believed that there was no need to address the constitutionality of §309. Justices Ginsburg, Breyer, and Souter dissented in opinions written by Justices Ginsburg and Breyer.

In their separate opinions, Justices Stevens, O'Connor, Ginsburg, and Breyer each addressed the petitioner's argument that §309 invokes gender stereotypes. The petitioner contended that §309 relies on the belief that an American father "remains aloof from day-to-day child rearing duties," and will not be as close to his child.[24] Justice Stevens, however, maintained that the statute has a non-stereotypical purpose of ensuring the existence of a blood relationship between father and child. Justice Stevens recognized that the distinction is reasonable because mothers have the opportunity to establish parentage at birth, while fathers do not always have that opportunity. Further, he contended that the distinction encourages the development of a healthy relationship between the citizen father and the foreign-born child, and fosters ties between the child and the United States. Thus, §309's additional requirements are appropriate for fathers, but unnecessary for mothers.

In their dissenting opinions, Justices Ginsburg and Breyer contended that §309 relies on generalizations about men and women and the ties they maintain with their children. Justice Ginsburg argued that §309's goals of assuring ties between the citizen father and the foreign-born child, and between the child and the United States can be achieved without reference to gender, while Justice Breyer argued similarly, positing a distinction between caretaker and non-caretaker parents, rather than mother and father.

In *Nguyen v. INS*, the Court considered a second challenge to §309.[25] The facts in *Nguyen* closely resembled those in *Miller*. Nguyen, the child of a citizen father and a non-citizen mother, born out of wedlock, challenged §309 on the grounds that its differing requirements for acquiring citizenship, based on the sex of the citizen parent, violated the Fifth Amendment's guarantee of equal protection.

A majority of the Court concluded that §309's differing requirements were justified by two important government objectives. First, the Court found that the government has an important interest in assuring that a biological parent-child relationship exists.[26] While a mother's relationship to a child may be established at birth or from hospital records, a father may not be present at the birth and may not be included on such records. In this way, the Court maintained, fathers and mothers are not similarly situated with regard to establishing biological parenthood.[27] Thus, a "different set of rules ... is neither surprising nor troublesome from a constitutional perspective."[28]

Second, the Court found that the government has an important government interest in ensuring that the child and the citizen parent have some demonstrated opportunity or potential to develop a relationship "that consists of the real, everyday ties that provide a connection between child and citizen parent and, in turn, the United States."[29] The opportunity for a meaningful relationship is presented to the mother at birth. However, the father is not assured of a similar opportunity. The Court concluded that §309 ensures that an opportunity for a meaningful relationship is presented to the father before citizenship is conferred upon his child.

As a result, the Court found that §309's differing requirements were substantially related to the important government interests. The Court noted that by linking citizenship to the child's youth, Congress promoted an opportunity for a parent-child relationship during the formative years of the child's life.[30] Alluding to its decision in *VMI*, the Court maintained that the fit between the §309 requirements and the important government interests was "exceedingly persuasive."[31]

Like the petitioner in *Miller*, Nguyen argued that §309 embodied a gender-based stereotype. However, the Court found that §309 addresses an "undeniable difference in the circumstance of the parents at the time a child is born."[32] This difference is not the result of a stereotype or "a frame of mind resulting from irrational or uncritical analysis."[33] Rather, §309 recognizes simply that at the moment of birth, the mother's knowledge of the child is established in a way not guaranteed to the unwed father.

While the Court's decisions involving sex and equal protection illustrate that it is concerned with the stereotyping of men and women, it is unclear whether it will continue to subject sex classifications and any related stereotypes to a traditional form of intermediate scrutiny. The Court's requirement of an "exceedingly persuasive justification" in *VMI* suggests that it may be interested in conducting a more exacting form of judicial review for sex classifications. In his *Miller* dissent, Justice Breyer emphasized the need to apply the standard established in *VMI*. However, in *Nguyen*, both the majority and the dissenting justices, in discussing an "exceeding persuasive justification," simply reiterated the traditional test that is used when applying intermediate scrutiny.[34] Thus, it is not clear whether sex classifications in future cases will be subject to a traditional form of intermediate scrutiny or some form of heightened scrutiny.

TITLE VII OF THE CIVIL RIGHTS ACT OF 1964

Title VII prohibits an employer from discriminating against any individual with respect to hiring or the terms and conditions of employment because of such individual's race, color, religion, sex, or national origin.[35] Title VII applies to a broad range of employment practices, including discrimination because of sex in hiring, placement, promotion, demotion, transfer, termination, and discipline. Because the statute prohibits sex discrimination with respect to all terms and conditions of employment, discrimination regarding salary, leave, and other benefits may also violate the act. Moreover, the statute's prohibition against sex discrimination extends to cover discrimination on the basis of pregnancy. This intention was clarified by Congress when it amended Title VII by enacting the Pregnancy Discrimination Act (PDA).[36]

In addition, the statute prohibits discrimination in referrals by employment agencies, actions by unions, and retaliation against employees for filing or participating in a Title VII claim or for opposing an employer's discriminatory practices. Title VII contains several exceptions to the prohibition against sex discrimination, the most important of which permits otherwise discriminatory conduct that satisfies a bona fide occupational qualification (BFOQ). Under §703(e)(1) of Title VII, an employer may discriminate on the basis of "religion, sex, or national origin in those certain instances where religion, sex, or national origin is a bona fide occupational qualification reasonably necessary to the normal operation of that particular business or enterprise."[37]

Although a wide variety of Title VII sex discrimination claims have been litigated in the courts, the major Supreme Court sex discrimination cases under Title VII have primarily focused on the following issues: pregnancy discrimination, gender stereotypes, mixed motives, sexual harassment, employer liability, retaliation, and class action status. These issues, as well as a discussion of the two different types of discrimination recognized under Title VII, are described below. This report, however, does not address pay discrimination claims brought under Title VII or the Equal Pay Act.

Disparate Treatment and Disparate Impact

The Court has developed two principal models for proving claims of employment discrimination. The "disparate treatment" model focuses on an employer's intent to discriminate. Alternately, the "disparate impact" model is concerned with the adverse effects of an employer's practices on a protected class. Under disparate impact analysis, a facially neutral employment practice may violate Title VII even if there is no evidence of an employer's intent to discriminate. To succeed, a plaintiff must demonstrate that the application of a specific employment practice has had a different effect on a particular group of employees.[38]

Both disparate treatment and disparate impact analyses involve a system of evidentiary burden shifting. Both models require the plaintiff to establish a prima facie case of discrimination.[39] If such a case can be established, the burden shifts to the employer to articulate a defense for its actions. For example, the employer may produce evidence showing that its actions are justified because of the needs of its business. Ultimately, however, the plaintiff retains the burden of persuasion; that is, the plaintiff must establish that the employer's assertion of a legitimate, nondiscriminatory reason for its actions was a pretext to obscure unlawful discrimination.[40]

Pregnancy Discrimination

In general, the Court has addressed Title VII and sex discrimination most frequently in the context of sexual harassment. However, the Court has also handed down a number of decisions involving pregnancy discrimination. For example, in one of its earliest cases, *General Electric Co. v. Gilbert*, the Court ruled that an employer's practice of excluding pregnant employees from receiving benefits under its temporary disability plan did not constitute sex discrimination in violation of Title VII.[41] Congress subsequently overruled the Court's decision by enacting the PDA, which amended Title VII to clarify that the statute's prohibition on discrimination in employment "on the basis of sex" includes discrimination "because of or on the basis of pregnancy, childbirth, or related medical conditions."[42] In addition, under the statute, "women affected by pregnancy, childbirth, or related medical conditions shall be treated the same for all employment-related purposes ... as other persons not so affected but similar in their ability or inability to work."[43]

In *UAW v. Johnson Controls*, the Court considered whether an employer may discriminate against fertile women because of its interest in protecting potential fetuses.[44] Johnson Controls, a battery manufacturer, implemented a policy that excluded "women who are pregnant or who are capable of bearing children" from jobs that exposed them to lead,[45] which was the primary ingredient in the manufacturing process at Johnson Controls. Although fertile women were excluded from employment, fertile men were still permitted to work. The Court found that Johnson Controls' policy was facially discriminatory because it did not apply to the reproductive capacity of the company's male employees in the same way it applied to that of female employees. The Court's conclusion was bolstered by the PDA.

Although Johnson Controls asserted that sex was a BFOQ for protecting fetal safety, the Court maintained that discrimination on the basis of sex for safety concerns is allowed only in narrow circumstances.[46] The Court stressed that to qualify as a BFOQ, an employment practice must relate to the essence or central mission of the employer's business.[47] Because reproductive capacity does not interfere with a woman's ability to perform work related to battery manufacturing, the Court rejected Johnson Controls' BFOQ defense.

In 2009, the Supreme Court issued a decision in *AT&T v. Hulteen*,[48] a pregnancy discrimination case that involved questions about whether women who took maternity leave before the PDA went into effect were entitled to protection. Prior to enactment of the PDA, AT&T had calculated pension benefits based on a seniority system that considered years of service minus uncredited leave, but had given less leave credit for pregnancy absences than for other types of medical leave. The plaintiffs claimed that, for purposes of calculating their current retirement and other benefits, they were entitled to retroactive credit for the time they spent on maternity leave, while the employer argued that they were not required to account for leave that took place before the PDA went into effect.

Ultimately, the Court ruled in favor of AT&T, ruling that its seniority system did not violate Title VII "when it gives current effect to such rules that operated before the PDA."[49] Under Title VII, it is not unlawful for an employer to provide different levels of benefits pursuant to a bona fide seniority system, as long as there is no intention to discriminate.[50] According to the Court, AT&T's pre-PDA seniority system did not reflect intentional sex discrimination because it was lawful at the time it was adopted. Therefore, the Court held that AT&T's pension calculations were made pursuant to a bona fide seniority system and were permissible under the statute.

In 2015, the Supreme Court issued a decision in *Young v. United Parcel Service*.[51] In the case, a United Parcel Service (UPS) worker named Peggy Young challenged her employer's refusal to grant her a light-duty work assignment while she was pregnant, claiming that UPS's actions violated the PDA. The dispute in *Young* centered on how to interpret the second clause of the PDA, which provides that pregnant workers must be treated the same "as other persons not so affected but similar in their ability or inability to work ... "[52] In her argument to the Court, Young contended that the PDA's second clause requires employers to accommodate workers disabled by pregnancy in the same way that they accommodate employees who are disabled in other ways but similar in their inability to work. In contrast, UPS argued that its policy did not violate the PDA because pregnant workers were treated the same as other workers who were disabled due to offthe-job injuries. In a 6-3 ruling, the Court rejected the arguments of both parties.

According to the Court, Young's interpretation of the statute would grant pregnant workers a "most-favored nation status" that would require employers who provided one or two employees with an accommodation to provide the same accommodation to all pregnant employees, regardless of any other relevant criteria, such as the nature of the jobs in question.[53] The Court rejected this approach as contrary to congressional intent, noting that disparate treatment law allows employers to establish policies that may negatively affect protected employees, subject to certain conditions. The Court also refused to defer to EEOC guidance that echoed Young's position, noting that the agency had altered its interpretation after the Court granted review in the case.[54] Likewise, the Court disagreed with UPS's interpretation because it would render the PDA's second clause "superfluous" and would be contrary to the unambiguous intent expressed by Congress when it overturned the *Gilbert* decision.[55]

Instead, the Court relied on an alternative interpretation of the PDA that appears to strike a middle ground between the approaches advocated by Young and UPS. Adapting the burden of proof framework established in the disparate treatment case of *McDonnell Douglas Corp. v. Green*,[56] the *Young* Court held that a pregnant worker who alleges a violation of the PDA's second clause when an employer denies her an accommodation must establish a prima facie case of discrimination by showing that she is a member of the protected class; that she sought an accommodation; that the employer denied the accommodation; and that the employer accommodated others similarly situated in their ability or inability to work.[57] At that point, the employer must show that it had a legitimate, nondiscriminatory reason for denying the accommodation, although the administrative convenience or expense of accommodating pregnant employees will not be deemed to be a legitimate excuse. Finally, the employee may rebut this claim by demonstrating that the employer's rationale is pretextual.[58]

Further, the Court ruled, an employee may reach a jury on the issue of pretext if she provides "sufficient evidence that the employer's policies impose a significant burden on pregnant workers, and that the employer's 'legitimate, nondiscriminatory' reasons are not sufficiently strong to justify the burden, but rather—when considered along with the burden imposed—give rise to an inference of intentional discrimination."[59] According to the Court, a pregnant employee can establish that a "significant burden" exists if she can demonstrate that an employer provides accommodations to a large percentage of non-pregnant workers but denies such accommodations to a large percentage of pregnant workers. Based on this reasoning, the Court vacated the lower court's judgment and remanded the case so that the court could determine "whether the nature of the employer's policy and the way in which it burdens pregnant women shows that the employer has engaged in intentional discrimination."[60] Although the Court did not rule on the merits of Young's claim, it did appear to indicate that she could meet her burden of proof by arguing that the "combined effects" of UPS's policies accommodating three separate categories of non-pregnant employees, while simultaneously refusing to accommodate the majority of pregnant employees, imposed a significant burden on the latter.[61] Ultimately, the Court's ruling preserves the ability of pregnant workers to sue under the PDA when an employer refuses to accommodate pregnancy-related disabilities, but it does not require employers to automatically provide accommodations under all circumstances.[62]

Gender Stereotypes

The Supreme Court has also ruled that employment decisions made on the basis of gender stereotypes may constitute unlawful sex discrimination. In *Price Waterhouse v. Hopkins*,[63] the plaintiff, a woman who was denied partnership in the accounting firm where she worked, was apparently rejected because of concerns about her interpersonal skills. Some of these concerns, however, appeared to reflect gender stereotypes. For example, one male partner referred to the plaintiff as "macho," and another informed her that she could improve her chances of making partner if she learned to "walk more femininely, talk more femininely, dress more femininely, wear make-up, have her hair styled, and wear jewelry."[64] Reasoning that sex stereotyping is a form of discrimination on the basis of sex, the Court found that employment decisions that result from sex stereotypes may violate Title VII.[65]

Although the decision was in part a victory for employees who have been victims of employment actions based on gender stereotypes, another aspect of the *Hopkins* ruling favored employers by requiring a lower standard of proof when employers defend their actions in mixed-motive cases. In mixed-motive cases such as *Hopkins*, there are both legitimate and illegitimate reasons for an employer's adverse employment action. In such cases, the Court held that employers may rebut an employee's showing that discrimination was a "motivating factor" in the adverse action by proving that they would have made the same decision even if discrimination had not been a factor. This holding made it easier for employers to defend against discrimination lawsuits by their employees.

Mixed Motives

As noted above, a mixed-motive employment discrimination case is a case in which the employer has both legitimate and illegitimate reasons for taking the challenged employment action. Several years after the Supreme Court ruled in the *Hopkins* case, Congress passed Title VII amendments that partially overturned the decision.[66] In the amendments, Congress added a provision that defined unlawful employment actions to include situations in which discrimination is "a motivating factor for any employment practice, even though other factors also motivated the practice."[67] If an employer violates this provision but establishes that it would have taken the same employment action absent the illegitimate motive, the amendments specify that courts may grant the plaintiff declaratory and injunctive relief, as well as attorneys' fees, although plaintiffs are not entitled to damages, hiring, reinstatement, or promotion.[68]

The Title VII amendments, however, did not address certain questions regarding the evidentiary burden of proof in mixed-motive cases. In 2003, the Supreme Court addressed the issue, ruling in *Desert Palace v. Costa* that direct evidence of discrimination is not required in mixed-motive cases.[69] By allowing plaintiffs to present circumstantial evidence of discrimination, the decision made it easier for employees to win in mixed-motive cases.

Sexual Harassment

Courts have recognized two forms of sexual harassment under Title VII. The first, quid pro quo sexual harassment, occurs when submission to unwelcome sexual advances or other conduct of a sexual nature is made a condition of an individual's employment or is otherwise used as the basis for employment decisions. The second form of harassment involves conduct that has the purpose or effect of interfering unreasonably with an individual's work performance or of creating a hostile or offensive working environment.[70] This second form of sexual harassment, which the Court first recognized as a cognizable claim in *Meritor Savings Bank, FSB v. Vinson*,[71] is referred to as "hostile environment" sexual harassment.

In *Harris v. Forklift Systems, Inc.*, the Court sought to define when a workplace was sufficiently "hostile" for purposes of maintaining a claim under Title VII.[72] The petitioner, a female manager at an equipment rental company, alleged that the company's president created a hostile environment by repeatedly insulting her because of her gender and making her the target of unwanted sexual innuendos.

The Court determined that an employee does not need to suffer injury to assert a hostile environment claim under Title VII: "So long as the environment would reasonably be perceived, and is perceived, as hostile or abusive ... there is no need for it also to be psychologically injurious."[73] The Court identified four factors that should be considered to determine whether a hostile environment exists: (1) the frequency of the discriminatory conduct; (2) the severity of such conduct; (3) whether the conduct is physically threatening or humiliating; and (4) whether the conduct interferes unreasonably with an employee's work performance.[74] Although the Court recognized these factors as those to be considered in identifying a hostile environment, it emphasized that no single factor is determinative.

Same-Sex Sexual Harassment

In 1998, the Court interpreted Title VII's prohibition against discrimination "because of ... sex" to include harassment involving a plaintiff and defendant of the same sex.[75] The petitioner in *Oncale v. Sundowner Offshore Services, Inc.* alleged that he was physically assaulted in a sexual manner and was threatened with rape by three male co-workers.[76] Two of the co-workers had supervisory authority over the petitioner.

Although the Court acknowledged that Congress was "assuredly" not concerned with male-onmale sexual harassment when it enacted Title VII, it found no justification in the statutory language or the Court's precedents for excluding same-sex harassment claims from the coverage of Title VII.[77] At the same time, the Court stated that inquiries in same-sex harassment cases require careful consideration of the social context in which particular behavior occurs and is experienced by the claimant. For example, the Court distinguished a football player being patted on the butt in a locker room from similar behavior occurring in an office. The Court contended that this kind of consideration would prevent Title VII from becoming a "general civility code" for the American workplace.[78]

Employer Liability

The Court continued its examination of hostile environment sexual harassment in two cases involving vicarious liability. In *Faragher v. City of Boca Raton*, the Court found that an employer is vicariously liable for actionable discrimination caused by a supervisor, subject to an affirmative defense that must consider the reasonableness of the employer's conduct, as well as the conduct of the employee.[79] The petitioner, a former lifeguard for the Marine Safety Section of Boca Raton's Parks and Recreation Department, alleged that she was subject to an environment characterized by lewd remarks, gender-biased speech, and uninvited and offensive touching by her former supervisors.

Recognizing that the authority conferred as a result of a supervisor's relationship with the employer allows the supervisor greater ability to act inappropriately, the Court concluded that an employer could be vicariously liable when a supervisor misuses that authority. As the Court noted, "When a person with supervisory authority discriminates in the terms and conditions of subordinates' employment, his actions necessarily draw upon his superior position over the people who report to him ... whereas an employee generally cannot check a supervisor's abusive conduct the same way that she might deal with abuse from a co-worker."[80]

While the Court recognized that there could be vicarious liability for the misuse of supervisory authority, it established the availability of an affirmative defense for employers. Under this affirmative defense, an employer could assert that it exercised reasonable care to prevent and correct any sexually harassing behavior or establish that the employee unreasonably failed to take advantage of any preventive or corrective opportunities provided by the employer. The Court believed that the employer's ability to assert such an affirmative defense was consistent with Title VII's objective of encouraging employers to prevent sexual harassment from occurring.[81]

After applying its new rules to the case at bar, the Court concluded that the city did not exercise reasonable care to prevent the supervisors' harassing conduct. Although the city maintained a policy against sexual harassment, it failed to disseminate that policy to beach employees. Further, the city made no attempt to monitor the conduct of the supervisors or assure employees that they could bypass harassing supervisors to register complaints.

The Court revisited the issue of vicarious liability for employers in *Burlington Industries v. Ellerth*, a companion case to *Faragher*.[82] In *Ellerth*, the Court maintained that an employer may be found vicariously liable for harassment by a supervisor even if the employee suffers no adverse, tangible job consequences.

The petitioner in *Ellerth* alleged that she was subjected to repeated offensive remarks and gestures by a mid-level manager who supervised the petitioner's immediate supervisor. On three occasions, the manager made remarks that could be construed as threats to deny the petitioner job benefits. For example, the manager encouraged the petitioner to "loosen up" because he "could make [her] life very hard or very easy at Burlington."[83] Although Burlington maintained a policy against sexual harassment, the petitioner did not inform anyone in authority about the manager's misconduct. Instead, the petitioner resigned from her position, providing reasons unrelated to the harassment. Three weeks after her resignation, the petitioner informed Burlington of her true reasons for leaving.

While the manager's threats suggested that the claim should be analyzed as a quid pro quo claim, the Court categorized it as a hostile environment claim because it involved only unfulfilled threats. After reviewing the petitioner's claim in terms similar to *Faragher*, the Court determined that the manager at Burlington also misused his supervisory authority. The Court concluded that Burlington should be given the opportunity to assert and prove an affirmative defense to liability.

The Court has also addressed the availability of punitive damages for violations of Title VII. In *Kolstad v. American Dental Association*,[84] the Court continued to build on its holdings in *Faragher* and *Ellerth* by concluding that although an employer may be vicariously liable for the misconduct of its supervisory employees, it will not be subject to punitive damages if it has made good faith efforts to comply with Title VII. The Court noted that subjecting employers that adopt antidiscrimination policies to punitive damages would undermine Title VII's objective of encouraging employers to prevent discrimination in the workplace.

In 2004, the Supreme Court considered the defenses, if any, that may be available to an employer against an employee's claim that she was forced to resign because of "intolerable" sexual harassment at the hands of a supervisor. As noted above, an employer may generally assert an affirmative defense to supervisory harassment under the Court's 1998 rulings in *Faragher* and *Ellerth*. The defense is not available, however, if the harassment includes a "tangible employment action," such as discharge or demotion. In *Pennsylvania State Police v. Suders*,[85] the plaintiff claimed the tangible adverse action was supervisory harassment so severe that it drove the employee to quit, a constructive discharge in effect. The Court, in an opinion by Justice Ginsburg, only Justice Thomas dissenting, accepted the theory of a constructive discharge as a tangible employment action, but it also set conditions under which the employer could assert an affirmative defense and avoid strict liability under Title VII of the 1964 Civil Rights Act.[86] The issue was key to determining the scope of employers' vicarious liability in "supervisory" sexual harassment cases alleging a hostile work environment.

In *Faragher* and *Ellerth*, the Court had sought to clarify the nature and scope of an employer's legal liability for the discriminatory and harassing conduct of its supervisors in Title VII cases. It held employers strictly liable for a sexually hostile work environment created by a supervisor, when the challenged discrimination or harassment results in a "tangible employment action."[87] But in the absence of such a "company act" the employer may raise an affirmative defense based on its having in place a reasonable remedial process and on the employee's failure to take advantage of it. Thus, the *Ellerth/Faragher* defense has two components: "(a) that the employer exercised reasonable care to prevent and correct promptly any sexually harassing behavior, and (b) that the plaintiff employee unreasonably failed to take advantage of any preventative or corrective opportunities provided by the employer or to avoid harm otherwise."[88]

The Supreme Court defined a "tangible employment action" categorically to mean any "significant change in employment status," that may—but not always—result in economic harm. Specifically, the term includes "hiring, firing, failing to promote, reassignment with significantly different responsibilities, or a decision causing a significant change in benefits"[89] However, a "constructive discharge," where the employee quits, claiming that conditions are so intolerable that he or she was effectively "fired," presented an unresolved issue. Could an employer, faced with a claim of constructive discharge, still assert the *Ellerth/Faragher* defense?

Ultimately, the Court held that Title VII encompasses employer liability for constructive discharge claims attributable to a supervisor, but ruled that an "employer does not have recourse to the *Ellerth/Faragher* affirmative defense when a supervisor's official act precipitates the constructive discharge; absent such a 'tangible employment action,' however, the defense is available to the employer whose supervisors are charged with harassment."[90] In recognizing hostile environment constructive discharge claims, *Suders* enhanced Title VII protection for employees who quit their jobs over intense sexual harassment by a supervisor. But the decision also makes it easier for an employer to defend against such claims by showing that it has reasonable procedures for reporting and correcting harassment of which the employee failed to avail herself. Only "if the plaintiff quits in reasonable response to an employer-sanctioned adverse action officially changing her employment status or situation, for example, a humiliating demotion, extreme cut in pay, or transfer to a position in which she would face unbearable working condition," is the employer made strictly liable for monetary damages or other Title VII relief.[91]

Moreover, even where there has been a tangible employment action, coupled with a constructive discharge or resignation, the employer may have defenses available. First, the employer may argue that the harassing conduct did not occur as alleged, or was not sufficiently severe, pervasive, or unwelcome to meet standards for a Title VII violation. Second, if the tangible employment action is shown to be unrelated to the alleged harassment, or is taken for legitimate non-discriminatory reasons—particularly, if by persons other than the alleged harasser—the employer might escape liability. Finally, the employer might be able to demonstrate that, whatever form the underlying supervisory harassment may take, it did not meet the standard for constructive discharge: "so intolerable that a reasonable person would have felt compelled to resign."[92] But *Suders* also makes it more difficult to obtain summary judgment and avoid jury trials in sexual harassment cases involving constructive discharge claims. Under the decision, if there is any real dispute about whether the employee suffered a tangible employment action, the employer may not rely on the affirmative defense to obtain summary judgment.

Retaliation

More recently, the Court has issued several decisions that have expanded the protections available under Title VII's anti-retaliation provision. In 2006, the Court issued its decision in *Burlington Northern & Santa Fe Railway Co. v. White*,[93] a case that involved questions about the scope of the retaliation provision under Title VII. In a 9-0 decision with one justice concurring, the Court held that the statute's retaliation provision encompasses any employer action that "would have been materially adverse to a reasonable employee or job applicant."[94] This standard, which is much broader than a standard that would have confined the retaliation provision to actions that affect only the terms and conditions of employment, generally makes it easier to sue employers if they retaliate against workers who complain about discrimination. Under the Court's interpretation, employees must establish only that the employer's actions might dissuade a worker from making a charge of discrimination. This means that an employee may successfully sue an employer for retaliation even if the employer's action does not actually result in an adverse employment action, such as being fired or losing wages.

In 2009, the Court issued a decision in *Crawford v. Metropolitan Government of Nashville and Davidson County*,[95] a case in which the plaintiff alleged that her participation in a sexual harassment investigation against her supervisor resulted in her termination. Although the plaintiff cooperated in the investigation and provided testimony regarding explicit comments and actions made by her boss, the fact that she had not filed the sexual harassment complaint or other charges with the Equal Employment Opportunity Commission (EEOC) led the lower court to rule that she was not covered under Title VII's retaliation provision. In reversing the decision, the Court held that Title VII's retaliation provision encompasses retaliation against "an employee who speaks out about discrimination not on her own initiative, but in answering questions during an employer's internal investigation."[96] The Court emphasized that this result would prevent employers from undermining the purpose of Title VII by silencing employees who might fear being penalized if they reported discrimination during the course of an investigation.

More recently, the Court ruled in *Thompson v. North American Stainless*,[97] a sex discrimination case involving the question of whether Title VII creates a cause of action for third-party retaliation for individuals who have not personally engaged in protected activity. In *Thompson*, the plaintiff, who was fired three weeks after his then-fiancée filed a discrimination claim with the EEOC, alleged that his termination constituted unlawful retaliation in violation of Title VII, while the employer claimed that his discharge was for reasons of performance. The en banc Sixth Circuit, in a fractured opinion, held that the employee was not protected because he had not opposed any practice nor participated in a proceeding as required by the anti-retaliation provision of Title VII.[98]

In a unanimous decision, the Court reversed, holding that it had "little difficulty" in concluding that the "firing of Thompson violated Title VII."[99] Citing *Burlington*'s holding that Title VII's anti-retaliation provision prohibits actions that might dissuade a reasonable worker from complaining of discrimination, the Court declared "it obvious that a reasonable worker might be dissuaded from engaging in protected activity if she knew that her fiancé would be fired."[100] The Court declined to establish fixed rules regarding the types of third-party relationships that are protected, but did indicate "that firing a close family member will almost always meet the *Burlington* standard, and inflicting a milder reprisal on a mere acquaintance will almost never do so...."[101]

Class Action Status

In *Wal-Mart v. Dukes*, the Supreme Court considered whether it was appropriate to approve class action status for up to 1.5 million current and former female employees of Wal-Mart retail stores nationwide. Alleging a pattern of sex discrimination, the plaintiffs claim that women were paid less than male workers in comparable positions and that the company systematically passed over female employees when awarding promotions to management. A federal district court certified the class.[102] Wal-Mart appealed the district court's class action certification, and a three-judge panel of the appellate court upheld the class action certification,[103] as did a subsequent ruling by a divided panel of appellate judges sitting en banc.[104] In a 5-4 decision, however, the Supreme Court reversed the class certification ruling.[105]

Under the Federal Rules of Civil Procedure, parties seeking class certification must show, among other things, that "(1) the class is so numerous that joinder of all members is impracticable, (2) there are questions of law or fact common to the class, (3) the claims or defenses of the representative parties are typical of the claims or defenses of the class, and (4) the representative parties will fairly and adequately protect the interests of the class."[106]

According to the Court, the *Wal-Mart* plaintiffs failed to meet the commonality requirement because they could not establish that Wal-Mart operated under a common, general policy of discrimination. Rather: "The only corporate policy that the plaintiffs' evidence convincingly establishes is Wal-Mart's 'policy' of allowing discretion by local supervisors over employment matters. On its face, of course, that is just the opposite of a uniform employment practice that would provide the commonality needed for a class action."[107]

In its ruling, the Court emphasized that plaintiffs must provide "significant proof" that a "specific employment practice" led to the discrimination, and rejected as insufficient statistical and anecdotal evidence offered by the plaintiffs.[108] Although the Court's decision makes it more difficult for employees to receive class certification and thus makes it less likely that large employers will face similar suits in the future, it is not the end of the litigation against Wal-Mart. The plaintiffs may still pursue their claims as individuals, or perhaps as part of a smaller class.

TITLE IX OF THE EDUCATION AMENDMENTS OF 1972

Title IX of the Education Amendments of 1972 prohibits discrimination on the basis of sex in educational programs and activities that receive federal funding. Until recently, Title IX claims have been most common among women and girls challenging inequities in sports programs,[109] but Title IX also provides a basis for challenging sexual harassment in classrooms and on campuses.

Title IX provides, in relevant part, that "[n]o person in the United States shall, on the basis of sex, be excluded from participation in, be denied the benefits of, or be subjected to discrimination under any education program or activity receiving Federal financial assistance.... "[110] The Court's recent decisions involving Title IX address various issues, including the availability of damages, the parties that are subject to liability, the scope of retaliation claims, and the availability of other statutory remedies.

In an early Title IX case, the Supreme Court held that the statute provides student victims with an avenue of judicial relief. In *Cannon v. University of Chicago*,[111] the Court ruled that an implied right of action exists under Title IX for student victims of sex discrimination who need not exhaust their administrative remedies before filing suit. However, the availability of monetary damages under Title IX remained uncertain until *Franklin v. Gwinnett County Public Schools.*[112] In *Franklin*, a female high school student brought an action for damages under Title IX against her school district alleging that she had been subjected to sexual harassment and abuse by a teacher. Although the harassment became known and an investigation was conducted, teachers and administrators did not act and the petitioner was subsequently discouraged from pressing charges. The Court, which found that sexual harassment by a teacher constituted discrimination on the basis of sex, held that damages were available to the sexual harassment victim if she could prove that the school district had intentionally violated Title IX.

After *Franklin*, it was clear that sexual harassment by a teacher constituted sex discrimination, but the extent to which school districts could be held liable for misconduct by its employees was less clear. The appropriate standard for measuring a school district's liability for sexual abuse of a student by a teacher remained unsettled until the Supreme Court ruling in *Gebser v. Lago Vista Independent School District.*[113] In *Gebser*, the Court determined that a school district will not be held liable under Title IX for a teacher's sexual harassment of a student if the school district did not have actual notice of the harassment and did not exhibit deliberate indifference to the misconduct.[114] The petitioner, a female high school student, was involved in a sexual relationship with one of her teachers. Unlike the situation in *Franklin*, the school district did not have actual notice of any sexual relationship between the petitioner and the teacher until they were discovered by a police officer. The principal of the petitioner's school did learn of inappropriate comments made by the teacher prior to the discovery, but he cautioned the teacher about such comments. After the sexual relationship became known, the school district quickly terminated the teacher. Despite the school district's actions, the petitioner argued that the school district should be found liable on the basis of vicarious liability or constructive notice.[115]

In requiring the school district to have actual notice of the harassment, the Court discussed the absence of an express cause of action under Title IX. Unlike Title VII, Title IX does not address damages or the particular situations in which damages are available.[116] While Title IX does address a denial of funds for noncompliance with its provisions, it does not provide for a private right of action. Instead, a private right of action has been judicially implied.[117]

Because Title IX does not contain any reference to the recovery of damages in private actions, the Court reasoned that its recognition of theories of vicarious liability and constructive notice would allow an unlimited recovery where Congress has not spoken.[118] Stated differently, the Court was reluctant to expand the availability of damages for such theories when Title IX failed to provide initially for a private cause of action. In this way, the Court sought to refine its holding in *Franklin* and limit those situations in which a remedy for damages would lie.

The Court believed that Title IX's remedial scheme would be undermined if it did not require that a school district have actual notice of a teacher's sexual harassment. Under Title IX, financial assistance will not be denied until the "appropriate person or persons" have been advised of the discrimination and have failed to end the discrimination voluntarily.[119] An "appropriate person" is an official of the entity receiving funds who has the authority to take corrective action.[120] Because the school district in *Gebser* did not have actual notice of the sexual relationship, it could not have taken any steps to end the alleged discrimination.

In addition, the Court stated that damages will not be available unless it is shown that a response exhibits a deliberate indifference to the discrimination; that is, there must be "an official decision by the recipient not to remedy the violation."[121] In *Gebser*, the school district responded to the situation by first cautioning the teacher, and then terminating him once the relationship was discovered. Thus, the Court concluded that the school district did not act with deliberate indifference.

Davis v. Monroe County Board of Education, decided in 1999, addressed the standard of liability that should be imposed on school districts to remedy student-on-student harassment.[122] The plaintiff in *Davis* alleged that her fifth-grade daughter had been harassed by another student over a prolonged period—a fact reported to teachers on several occasions—but that school officials had failed to take corrective action. Justice O'Connor, writing for a sharply divided Court, determined that the plaintiff had stated a Title IX claim.

Because the statute restricts the actions of federal grant recipients, however, and not the conduct of third parties, the Court again refused to impose vicarious liability on the school district. Instead, "a recipient of federal funds may be liable in damages under Title IX only for its own misconduct."[123] School authorities' own "deliberate indifference" to student-on-student harassment could violate Title IX in certain cases. Thus, the Court held, where officials have "actual knowledge" of the harassment, where the "harasser is under the school's disciplinary authority," and where the harassment is so severe "that it can be said to deprive the victims of access to the educational opportunities or benefits provided by the school," the district may be held liable for damages under Title IX.[124]

While the development of sex discrimination law under Title IX owes much to Title VII, the *Davis* Court's recognition of student-on-student harassment highlights dramatic differences between the two statutes. Indeed, in qualifying the *Davis* standard, the Court suggested that student harassment may be far more difficult to prove than sexual harassment in employment. Beyond requiring "actual knowledge," Justice O'Connor cautioned that "schools are unlike adult workplaces" and disciplinary decisions of school administrators are not to be "second guess[ed]" by lower courts unless "clearly unreasonable" under the circumstances. Additionally, the majority emphasized that "[d]amages are not available for simple acts of teasing and name-calling among school children, even where these comments target differences in gender."[125] In effect, *Davis* left to school administrators the task of drawing the line between innocent teasing and actionable sexual harassment—a difficult and legally perilous task at best.

In a separate decision the same year, the Court found that a private organization is not subject to Title IX simply because it receives payments from entities that receive federal financial assistance. In *National Collegiate Athletic Association v. Smith*,[126] the respondent, a female graduate student, alleged that the National Collegiate Athletic Association (NCAA) discriminated against her on the basis of sex by denying her permission to play intercollegiate volleyball at two federally assisted institutions. Under NCAA rules, a graduate student is permitted to participate in intercollegiate athletics only at the institution that awarded her undergraduate degree. The respondent, who was enrolled at two different universities for her graduate degree, argued that the NCAA granted more waivers from eligibility restrictions to male graduate students than to female graduate students.

The Court concluded that the NCAA was not a recipient of Title IX funds because the NCAA did not receive federal assistance either directly or through an intermediary. Instead, it received dues payments from member institutions. The Court stated, "[a]t most, the Association's receipt of dues demonstrates that it indirectly benefits from the federal assistance afforded its members. This showing, without more, is insufficient to trigger Title IX coverage."[127] Because the Court found that the NCAA was not amenable to suit, it did not address the respondent's substantive allegations of discrimination.

In 2005, the Court handed down its decision in *Jackson v. Birmingham Board of Education*,[128] a case that further broadened the scope of Title IX to include protection against retaliation. In this case, which involved a girls' basketball coach who claimed that he was removed from his coaching position in retaliation for his complaints about unequal treatment of the girl's team, the Court held that Title IX not only encompasses retaliation claims, but also is available to individuals who complain about sex discrimination, even if such individuals themselves are not the direct victims of sex discrimination.[129] Reasoning that "Title IX's enforcement scheme would unravel" "if retaliation were not prohibited,"[130] the Court concluded that "when a funding recipient retaliates against a person because he complains of sex discrimination, this constitutes intentional discrimination on the basis of sex in violation of Title IX."[131]

More recently, the Court issued a decision in *Fitzgerald v. Barnstable School Committee*,[132] a case in which the Court considered whether Title IX provides the exclusive statutory remedy for unlawful sex discrimination in the education context. The lower court, concluding that Title IX was the exclusive statutory remedy, had rejected a claim that the original plaintiffs filed under 42 U.S.C. §1983 for violations of Title IX and the Equal Protection Clause of the Constitution.[133] In a unanimous decision, the Court reversed, holding that "Title IX was not meant to be an exclusive mechanism for addressing gender discrimination in schools, or a substitute for § 1983 suits as a means of enforcing constitutional rights."[134] As a result, plaintiffs may file claims related to sex discrimination in education under both statutes in the future.

End Notes

[1] U.S. Const. amend. XIV, §1; U.S. Const. amend. V.

[2] 42 U.S.C. §§2000e et seq.

[3] 20 U.S.C. §§1681 et seq.

[4] U.S. Const. amend. XIV, §1 (emphasis added).

[5] Tigner v. Texas, 310 U.S. 141, 147 (1940).

[6] See Ferguson v. Skrupa, 372 U.S. 726, 732 (1963).

[7] See e.g., San Antonio Indep. Sch. Dist. v. Rodriguez, 411 U.S. 1 (1973).

[8] Craig v. Boren, 429 U.S. 190, 197 (1976). In U.S. v. Virginia, the Court required the Commonwealth of Virginia to provide an "exceedingly persuasive justification" for its policy of maintaining an all-male military academy. 518 U.S. 515 (1996). It is unclear whether this standard differs from the intermediate scrutiny standard of review. See infra text accompanying notes 16-34.

[9] See e.g., Lindsley v. Nat'l Carbonic Gas Co., 220 U.S. 61 (1911); Royster Guano Co. v. Virginia, 253 U.S. 412 (1920); San Antonio Indep. Sch. Dist. v. Rodriguez, 411 U.S. 1 (1973); Mass. Bd. of Ret. v. Murgia, 427 U.S. 307 (1976); Maher v. Roe, 432 U.S. 464 (1977).

[10] 429 U.S. 190 (1976).

[11] Id. at 198.

[12] See, e.g., Califano v. Goldfarb, 430 U.S. 199 (1977) (invalidating section of the Social Security Act that permitted survivors' benefits for widowers only if they were receiving half of their support from their wives); Orr v. Orr, 440 U.S. 268 (1979) (invalidating Alabama statute that imposed alimony obligations on husbands, but not wives); Caban v. Mohammed, 441 U.S. 380 (1979) (invalidating New York statute that required the consent of the mother, but not the father, to permit the adoption of an illegitimate child); Mississippi University for Women v. Hogan, 458 U.S. 718 (1982) (invalidating policy of a state-supported university that limited admission to its nursing school to women on the grounds that it reinforced traditional stereotypes).

[13] 511 U.S. 127, 129 (1994).

[14] Id. at 132.

[15] Id. at 140.

[16] 518 U.S. 515 (1996).

[17] Id.

[18] Id. at 540.

[19] Id. at 533.

[20] Id. at 549.

[21] 523 U.S. 420 (1998).

[22] 8 U.S.C. §1409.

[23] Miller, 523 U.S. at 441.

[24] Id. at 443.

[25] 533 U.S. 53 (2001).

[26] Id. at 62.

[27] Id. at 63.

[28] Id.

[29] Id. at 65.

[30] Id. at 68-69.

[31] Id. at 70.

[32] Id. at 68.

[33] Id.

[34] See, e.g., id. at 70 ("We have explained that an 'exceedingly persuasive justification' is established 'by showing at least that the classification serves 'important governmental objectives and that the discriminatory means employed' are 'substantially related to the achievement of those objectives.' "); id. at 74 ("Because the Immigration and Naturalization Service (INS) has not shown an exceedingly persuasive justification for the sex based classification embodied in 8 U.S.C. § 1409(a)(4)—i.e., because it has failed to establish at

least that the classification substantially relates to the achievement of important governmental objectives—I would reverse the judgment of the Court of Appeals.").

[35] 42 U.S.C. §§2000e et seq.

[36] 42 U.S.C. §2000e(k).

[37] 42 U.S.C. §2000e-2(e)(1).

[38] See Griggs v. Duke Power Co., 401 U.S. 424 (1971).

[39] A prima facie case is a case that contains elements that are sufficient to establish a claim unless disproved.

[40] See, McDonnell Douglas Corp. v. Green, 411 U.S. 792 (1973).

[41] 429 U.S. 125 (1976).

[42] 42 U.S.C. §2000e(k). The statute does contain a narrow exception if an employer can establish that having a nonpregnant employee is a "bona fide occupational qualification that is reasonably necessary to the normal operation of that particular business or enterprise." 42 U.S.C. §2000e-2(e).

[43] 42 U.S.C. §2000e(k).

[44] 499 U.S. 187 (1991).

[45] Id. at 192.

[46] Johnson Controls, 499 U.S. at 202.

[47] See, e.g., Dothard v. Rawlinson, 433 U.S. 321 (1977) (finding sex to be a BFOQ because the employment of a female guard in a maximum-security male penitentiary could create a risk of violence and jeopardize the safety of inmates); Western Airlines, Inc. v. Criswell, 472 U.S. 400 (1985) (finding age to be a BFOQ in an ADEA case because the employment of an older flight engineer could cause a safety emergency and jeopardize the safety of passengers).

[48] 556 U.S. 701 (2009).

[49] Id. at 708.

[50] 42 U.S.C. §2000e-2(h).

[51] 135 S. Ct. 1338 (2015).

[52] 42 U.S.C. §2000e(k).

[53] Young v. UPS, 135 S. Ct. 1338, 1349 (2015).

[54] Id. at 1351-52.

[55] Id. at 1352-53.

[56] 411 U.S. 792 (1973).

[57] Young, 135 S. Ct. at 1354.

[58] Id.

[59] Id.

[60] Id. at 1344.

[61] Id. at 1354-55.

[62] However, the significance of the Court's decision may be limited by changes that were made to the Americans with Disabilities Act (ADA) during the course of litigation. P.L. 110-325, §4(a). The EEOC subsequently issued guidance that appears likely to make it significantly easier for a pregnant employee subject to a temporary lifting restriction to establish a disability claim under the ADA in the future. 29 C.F.R. §1630.2(j)(1)(ix) App. For a more detailed discussion of the Young case, see CRS Report R44204, The Pregnancy Discrimination Act and the Supreme Court: A Legal Analysis of Young v. United Parcel Service, by Jody Feder.

[63] 490 U.S. 228 (1989).

[64] Id. at 234-35.

[65] Id. at 250-51.
[66] Civil Rights Act of 1991, P.L. 102-166, §107(a).
[67] 42 U.S.C. §2000e-2(m).
[68] Id. at §2000e-5(g)(2).
[69] 539 U.S. 90 (2003).
[70] For detailed information on sexual harassment, see CRS Report RL33736, Sexual Harassment: Developments in Federal Law, by Jody Feder.
[71] 477 U.S. 57 (1986).
[72] 510 U.S. 17 (1993).
[73] Id. at 22.
[74] Id. at 23.
[75] 42 U.S.C. §2000e-2.
[76] 523 U.S. 75, 77 (1998).
[77] Id. at 79.
[78] Id. at 80.
[79] 524 U.S. 775 (1998).
[80] Id. at 803.
[81] Id. at 805.
[82] 524 U.S. 742 (1998).
[83] Id. at 748.
[84] 527 U.S. 526 (1999).
[85] 542 U.S. 129 (2004).
[86] 42 U.S.C. §§2000e et seq.
[87] 524 U.S. 742, 765 (1998); 524 U.S. 775, 807 (1998).
[88] Suders, 542 U.S. at 137-38.
[89] Ellerth, 524 U.S. at 761.
[90] Suders, 542 U.S. at 140-141.
[91] Id. at 209.
[92] Id. at 147.
[93] 548 U.S. 53 (2006).
[94] Id. at 57.
[95] 555 U.S. 271 (2009).
[96] Id. at 273.
[97] 562 U.S. 170 (2011).
[98] 567 F.3d 804, 816 (6th Cir. 2009).
[99] Thompson v. N. Am. Stainless, LP, 562 U.S. at 173. The Court also held that Thompson is an aggrieved person within the meaning of Title VII and therefore has standing to sue. Id. at 178.
[100] Id. at 174.
[101] Id. at 175.
[102] Dukes et al. v. Wal-Mart Stores, Inc., 222 F.R.D. 137 (N.D.Cal. 2004).
[103] Dukes v. Wal-Mart, 509 F.3d 1168 (9th Cir. 2007).
[104] Dukes v. Wal-Mart Stores, Inc., 603 F.3d 571 (9th Cir. 2010).
[105] 131 S. Ct. 2541 (2011). The Court also unanimously held that claims for monetary relief may not be certified pursuant to Rule 23(b)(2), unless the monetary relief is incidental to the injunctive or declaratory relief. Id. at 2557.
[106] Fed. R. Civ. P. 23(a).
[107] Wal-Mart, 131 S. Ct. at 2554.

[108] Id. at 2553-56.

[109] See CRS Report RL31709, Title IX, Sex Discrimination, and Intercollegiate Athletics: A Legal Overview, by Jody Feder.

[110] 20 U.S.C. §1681(a).

[111] 441 U.S. 677 (1979).

[112] 503 U.S. 60 (1992).

[113] 524 U.S. 274 (1998).

[114] Id.

[115] Under a theory of constructive notice, liability would be established on the grounds that the school district knew or should have known about the harassment, but failed to discover and eliminate it.

[116] Gebser, 24 U.S. at 283-84.

[117] See Cannon v. University of Chicago, 441 U.S. 677 (1979). A private right of action allows an individual to sue in court for violations under a statute rather than wait for a federal agency to pursue a complaint administratively.

[118] Gebser, 524 U.S. at 286.

[119] 20 U.S.C. §1682.

[120] Gebser, 524 U.S. at 290.

[121] Id.

[122] 526 U.S. 629 (1999).

[123] Id. at 640.

[124] Id. at 650.

[125] Id. at 648-52.

[126] 525 U.S. 459 (1999).

[127] Id. at 468.

[128] 544 U.S. 167 (2005).

[129] Id. at 171.

[130] Id. at 180.

[131] Id. at 174 (internal quotations omitted).

[132] 555 U.S. 246 (2009).

[133] 42 U.S.C. §1983, which provides a remedy for deprivation of rights under color of state law, creates no new substantive rights but rather provides relief where state law is inadequate. Thus, individuals who sue under §1983 must find a source of rights elsewhere. As a result, §1983 is often used to enforce constitutional rights, such as the right to equal protection.

[134] Fitzgerald, 555 U.S. at 258.

In: Pregnancy Discrimination
Editor: Dale Pittman

ISBN: 978-1-63485-489-4

Chapter 3

DECISION OF THE SUPREME COURT OF THE UNITED STATES IN THE CASE OF *YOUNG V. UNITED PARCEL SERVICE*, INC.*

(Slip Opinion) October Term, 2014

Syllabus

NOTE: Where it is feasible, a syllabus (headnote) will be released, as is being done in connection with this case, at the time the opinion is issued. The syllabus constitutes no part of the opinion of the Court but has been prepared by the Reporter of Decisions for the convenience of the reader. See *United States* v. *Detroit Timber & Lumber Co.,* 200 U. S. 321, 337

* This is an edited, reformatted and augmented version of the official slip opinion as delivered by the U.S. Supreme Court on March 25, 2014.

SUPREME COURT OF THE UNITED STATES

Syllabus

Young *v*. United Parcel Service, INC.

Certiorari to the United States Court of Appeals for the Fourth Circuit

No. 12–1226. Argued December 3, 2014—Decided March 25, 2015

The Pregnancy Discrimination Act added new language to the definitions subsection of Title VII of the Civil Rights Act of 1964. The first clause of the Pregnancy Discrimination Act specifies that Title VII's prohibition against sex discrimination applies to discrimination "because of or on the basis of pregnancy, childbirth, or related medical conditions." 42 U. S. C §2000e(k). The Act's second clause says that employers must treat "women affected by pregnancy . . . the same for all employment-related purposes . . . as other persons not so affected but similar in their ability or inability to work." *Ibid.* This case asks the Court to determine how the latter provision applies in the context of an employer's policy that accommodates many, but not all, workers with non-pregnancy-related disabilities.

Petitioner Young was a part-time driver for respondent United Parcel Service (UPS). When she became pregnant, her doctor advised her that she should not lift more than 20 pounds. UPS, however, required drivers like Young to be able to lift up to 70 pounds. UPS told Young that she could not work while under a lifting restriction. Young subsequently filed this federal lawsuit, claiming that UPS acted unlawfully in refusing to accommodate her pregnancy-related lifting restriction. She brought only a disparate-treatment claim of discrimination, which a plaintiff can prove either by direct evidence that a workplace policy, practice, or decision relies expressly on a protected characteristic, or by using the burden-shifting framework set forth in *McDonnell Douglas Corp.* v. *Green*, 411 U. S. 792. Under that framework, the plaintiff has "the initial burden" of "establishing a prima facie case" of discrimination. *Id.,* at 802. If she carries her burden, the employer must have an opportunity "to articulate some legitimate, non-discriminatory reason[s] for" the difference in treatment. *Ibid.* If the employer articulates such reasons, the plaintiff then has "an opportunity to prove by a preponderance of the evidence that the reasons . . . were a pretext for discrimination." *Texas Dept. of Community Affairs* v. *Burdine*, 450 U. S. 248, 253.

After discovery, UPS sought summary judgment. In reply, Young presented several favorable facts that she believed she could prove. In particular, she pointed to UPS policies that accommodated workers who were injured on the job, had disabilities covered by the Americans with Disabilities Act of 1990 (ADA), or had lost Department of Transportation (DOT) certifications. Pursuant to these policies, Young contended, UPS had accommodated several individuals whose disabilities created work restrictions similar to hers. She argued that these policies showed that UPS discriminated against its pregnant employees because it had a light-duty-for-injury policy for numerous "other persons," but not for pregnant workers. UPS responded that, since Young did not fall within the on-the-job injury, ADA, or DOT categories, it had not discriminated against Young on the basis of pregnancy, but had treated her just as it treated all "other" relevant "persons."

The District Court granted UPS summary judgment, concluding, *inter alia,* that Young could not make out a prima facie case of discrimination under *McDonnell Douglas*. The court found that those with whom Young had compared herself—those falling within the on-the-job, DOT, or ADA categories—were too different to qualify as "similarly situated comparator[s]." The Fourth Circuit affirmed.

Held:

1. An individual pregnant worker who seeks to show disparate treatment through indirect evidence may do so through application of the *McDonnell Douglas* framework. Pp. 10–23.
   (a) The parties' interpretations of the Pregnancy Discrimination Act's second clause are unpersuasive. Pp. 12–20.
      (i) Young claims that as long as "an employer accommodates only a subset of workers with disabling conditions," "pregnant workers who are similar in the ability to work [must] receive the same treatment even if still other nonpregnant workers do not receive accommodations." Brief for Petitioner 28. Her reading proves too much. The Court doubts that Congress intended to grant pregnant workers an unconditional "most-favored-nation" status, such that employers who provide one or two workers with an accommodation must provide similar accommodations to *all* pregnant workers, irrespective of any other criteria. After all, the second clause of the Act, when referring to nonpregnant persons with similar disabilities, uses the open-ended term

"other persons." It does not say that the employer must treat pregnant employees the "same" as "*any* other persons" who are similar in their ability or inability to work, nor does it specify the particular "other persons" Congress had in mind as appropriate comparators for pregnant workers. Moreover, disparate-treatment law normally allows an employer to implement policies that are not intended to harm members of a protected class, even if their implementation sometimes harms those members, as long as the employer has a legitimate, nondiscriminatory, nonpretextual reason for doing so. See, *e.g., Burdine*, *supra,* at 252–258. There is no reason to think Congress intended its language in the Pregnancy Discrimination Act to deviate from that approach. Pp. 12–14.

(ii) The Solicitor General argues that the Court should give special, if not controlling, weight to a 2014 Equal Employment Opportunity Commission guideline concerning the application of Title VII and the ADA to pregnant employees. But that guideline lacks the timing, "consistency," and "thoroughness" of "consideration" necessary to "give it power to persuade." *Skidmore* v. *Swift & Co.*, 323 U. S. 134, 140. The guideline was promulgated after certiorari was granted here; it takes a position on which previous EEOC guidelines were silent; it is inconsistent with positions long advocated by the Government; and the EEOC does not explain the basis for its latest guidance. Pp. 14–17.

(iii) UPS claims that the Act's second clause simply defines sex discrimination to include pregnancy discrimination. But that cannot be right, as the first clause of the Act accomplishes that objective. Reading the Act's second clause as UPS proposes would thus render the first clause superfluous. It would also fail to carry out a key congressional objective in passing the Act. The Act was intended to overturn the holding and the reasoning of *General Elec. Co.* v. *Gilbert*, 429 U. S. 125, which upheld against a Title VII challenge a company plan that provided nonoccupational sickness and accident benefits to all employees but did not provide disability-benefit payments for any absence due to pregnancy. Pp. 17–20.

(b) An individual pregnant worker who seeks to show disparate treatment may make out a prima facie case under the *McDonnell Douglas* framework by showing that she belongs to the protected class, that she sought accommodation, that the employer did not accommodate her, and that the employer did accommodate others "similar in their ability or inability to work." The employer may then seek to justify its refusal to accommodate the plaintiff by relying on "legitimate, nondiscriminatory" reasons for denying accommodation. That reason normally cannot consist simply of a claim that it is more expensive or less convenient to add pregnant women to the category of those whom the employer accommodates. If the employer offers a "legitimate, nondiscriminatory" reason, the plaintiff may show that it is in fact pretextual. The plaintiff may reach a jury on this issue by providing sufficient evidence that the employer's policies impose a significant burden on pregnant workers, and that the employer's "legitimate, nondiscriminatory" reasons are not sufficiently strong to justify the burden, but rather—when considered along with the burden imposed—give rise to an inference of intentional discrimination. The plaintiff can create a genuine issue of material fact as to whether a significant burden exists by providing evidence that the employer accommodates a large percentage of nonpregnant workers while failing to accommodate a large percentage of pregnant workers. This approach is consistent with the longstanding rule that a plaintiff can use circumstantial proof to rebut an employer's apparently legitimate, nondiscriminatory reasons, see *Burdine*, *supra*, at 255, n. 10, and with Congress' intent to overrule *Gilbert*. Pp. 20–23.

2. Under this interpretation of the Act, the Fourth Circuit's judgment must be vacated. Summary judgment is appropriate when there is "no genuine dispute as to any material fact." Fed. Rule Civ. Proc. 56(a). The record here shows that Young created a genuine dispute as to whether UPS provided more favorable treatment to at least some employees whose situation cannot reasonably be distinguished from hers. It is left to the Fourth Circuit to determine on remand whether Young also created a genuine issue of material fact as to whether UPS' reasons for having treated Young less favorably than these other nonpregnant employees were pretextual. Pp. 23–24.

707 F. 3d 437, vacated and remanded.

BREYER, J., delivered the opinion of the Court, in which ROBERTS, C. J., and GINSBURG, SOTOMAYOR, and KAGAN, JJ., joined. ALITO, J., filed an opinion concurring in the judgment. SCALIA, J., filed a dissenting opinion, in which KENNEDY and THOMAS, JJ., joined. KENNEDY, J., filed a dissenting opinion.

Opinion of the Court

NOTICE: This opinion is subject to formal revision before publication in the preliminary print of the United States Reports. Readers are requested to notify the Reporter of Decisions, Supreme Court of the United States, Washington, D. C. 20543, of any typographical or other formal errors, in order that corrections may be made before the preliminary print goes to press.

SUPREME COURT OF THE UNITED STATES

No. 12–1226

Peggy Young, Petitioner v. United Parcel Service, INC.

On Writ of Certiorari to the United States Court of Appeals for the Fourth Circuit

[March 25, 2015]

JUSTICE BREYER delivered the opinion of the Court.

The Pregnancy Discrimination Act makes clear that Title VII's prohibition against sex discrimination applies to discrimination based on pregnancy. It also says that employers must treat "women affected by pregnancy . . . the same for all employment-related purposes . . . as other persons not so affected but similar in their ability or inability to work." 42 U. S. C. §2000e(k). We must decide how this latter provision applies in the context of an employer's policy that accommodates many, but not all, workers with nonpregnancy-related disabilities.

In our view, the Act requires courts to consider the extent to which an employer's policy treats pregnant workers less favorably than it treats nonpregnant workers similar in their ability or inability to work. And here—as in all cases in which an individual plaintiff seeks to show disparate treatment through indirect evidence—it requires courts to consider any legitimate, nondiscriminatory, nonpretextual justification for these differences in treatment. See *McDonnell Douglas Corp.* v. *Green*, 411 U. S. 792, 802 (1973). Ultimately the court must determine whether the nature of the employer's policy and the way in which it burdens pregnant women shows that the employer has engaged in intentional discrimination. The Court of Appeals here affirmed a grant of summary judgment in favor of the employer. Given our view of the law, we must vacate that court's judgment.

I

A

We begin with a summary of the facts. The petitioner, Peggy Young, worked as a part-time driver for the respondent, United Parcel Service (UPS). Her responsibilities included pickup and delivery of packages that had arrived by air carrier the previous night. In 2006, after suffering several miscarriages, she became pregnant. Her doctor told her that she should not lift more than 20 pounds during the first 20 weeks of her pregnancy or more than 10 pounds thereafter. App. 580. UPS required drivers like Young to be able to lift parcels weighing up to 70 pounds (and up to 150 pounds with assistance). *Id.*, at 578. UPS told Young she could not work while under a lifting restriction. Young consequently stayed home without pay during most of the time she was pregnant and eventually lost her employee medical coverage.

Young subsequently brought this federal lawsuit. We focus here on her claim that UPS acted unlawfully in refusing to accommodate her pregnancy-related lifting restriction. Young said that her co-workers were willing to help her with heavy packages. She also said that UPS accommodated other drivers who were "similar in their . . .inability to work." She accordingly concluded that UPS must accommodate her as well. See Brief for Petitioner 30–31.

UPS responded that the "other persons" whom it had accommodated were (1) drivers who had become disabled on the job, (2) those who had lost their Department of Transportation (DOT) certifications, and (3) those who suffered from a disability covered by the Americans with Disabilities Act of 1990 (ADA), 104 Stat. 327, 42 U. S. C. §12101 *et seq.* UPS said that, since Young did not fall within any of those categories, it had not discriminated against

Young on the basis of pregnancy but had treated her just as it treated all "other" relevant "persons." See Brief for Respondent 34.

B

Title VII of the Civil Rights Act of 1964 forbids a covered employer to "discriminate against any individual with respect to . . . terms, conditions, or privileges of employment, because of such individual's . . . sex." 78 Stat. 253, 42 U. S. C. §2000e–2(a)(1). In 1978, Congress enacted the Pregnancy Discrimination Act, 92 Stat. 2076, which added new language to Title VII's definitions subsection. The first clause of the 1978 Act specifies that Title VII's "ter[m] 'because of sex' . . . include[s] . . . because of or on the basis of pregnancy, childbirth, or related medical conditions." §2000e(k). The second clause says that

> "women affected by pregnancy, childbirth, or related medical conditions shall be treated the same for all employment-related purposes . . . as other persons not so affected but similar in their ability or inability to work . . . ." *Ibid.*

This case requires us to consider the application of the second clause to a "disparate-treatment" claim—a claim that an employer intentionally treated a complainant less favorably than employees with the "complainant's qualifications" but outside the complainant's protected class. *McDonnell Douglas*, *supra*, at 802. We have said that "[l]iability in a disparate-treatment case depends on whether the protected trait actually motivated the employer's decision." *Raytheon Co.* v. *Hernandez*, 540 U. S. 44, 52 (2003) (ellipsis and internal quotation marks omitted). We have also made clear that a plaintiff can prove disparate treatment either (1) by direct evidence that a workplace policy, practice, or decision relies expressly on a protected characteristic, or (2) by using the burden-shifting framework set forth in *McDonnell Douglas*. See *Trans World Airlines, Inc.* v. *Thurston*, 469 U. S. 111, 121 (1985).

In *McDonnell Douglas,* we considered a claim of discriminatory hiring. We said that, to prove disparate treatment, an individual plaintiff must "carry the initial burden" of "establishing a prima facie case" of discrimination by showing

> "(i) that he belongs to a . . . minority; (ii) that he ap- plied and was qualified for a job for which the employer was seeking applicants; (iii)

> that, despite his qualifications, he was rejected; and (iv) that, after his rejection, the position remained open and the employer continued to seek applicants from persons of com- plainant's qualifications." 411 U. S., at 802.

If a plaintiff makes this showing, then the employer must have an opportunity "to articulate some legitimate, non-discriminatory reason for" treating employees outside the protected class better than employees within the protected class. *Ibid.* If the employer articulates such a reason, the plaintiff then has "an opportunity to prove by a preponderance of the evidence that the legitimate reasons offered by the defendant [*i.e.*, the employer] were not its true reasons, but were a pretext for discrimination." *Texas Dept. of Community Affairs* v. *Burdine*, 450 U. S. 248, 253 (1981).

We note that employment discrimination law also creates what is called a "disparate-impact" claim. In evaluating a disparate-impact claim, courts focus on the *effects* of an employment practice, determining whether they are unlawful irrespective of motivation or intent. See *Raytheon*, *supra*, at 52–53; see also *Ricci* v. *DeStefano*, 557 U. S. 557, 578 (2009). But Young has not alleged a disparateimpact claim.

Nor has she asserted what we have called a "pattern-or-practice" claim. See *Teamsters* v. *United States*, 431 U. S. 324, 359 (1977) (explaining that Title VII plaintiffs who allege a "pattern or practice" of discrimination may establish a prima facie case by "another means"); see also *id.*, at 357 (rejecting contention that the "burden of proof in a pattern-or-practice case must be equivalent to that outlined in *McDonnell Douglas*").

C

In July 2007, Young filed a pregnancy discrimination charge with the Equal Employment Opportunity Commission (EEOC). In September 2008, the EEOC provided her with a right-to-sue letter. See 29 CFR §1601.28 (2014). Young then filed this complaint in Federal District Court. She argued, among other things, that she could show by direct evidence that UPS had intended to discriminate against her because of her pregnancy and that, in any event, she could establish a prima facie case of disparate treatment under the *McDonnell Douglas* framework. See App. 60–62.

After discovery, UPS filed a motion for summary judgment. See Fed. Rule Civ. Proc. 56(a). In reply, Young pointed to favorable facts that she believed were either undisputed or that, while disputed, she could prove. They include the following:

1. Young worked as a UPS driver, picking up and delivering packages carried by air. Plaintiff 's Memorandum in Opposition to Defendant's Motion for Summary Judgment in No. 08–cv–02586 (D Md.), pp. 3–4 (hereinafter Memorandum).
2. Young was pregnant in the fall of 2006. *Id.,* at 15–16.
3. Young's doctor recommended that she "not be required to lift greater than 20 pounds for the first 20 weeks of pregnancy and no greater than 10 pounds thereafter." App. 580; see also Memorandum 17.
4. UPS required drivers such as Young to be able to "[l]ift, lower, push, pull, leverage and manipulate . . . packages weighing up to 70 pounds" and to "[a]ssist in moving packages weighing up to 150 pounds." App. 578; see also Memorandum 5.
5. UPS' occupational health manager, the official "responsible for most issues relating to employee health and ability to work" at Young's UPS facility, App. 568–569, told Young that she could not return to work during her pregnancy because she could not satisfy UPS' lifting requirements, see Memorandum 17−18; 2011 WL 665321, *5 (D Md., Feb. 14, 2011).
6. The manager also determined that Young did not qualify for a temporary alternative work assignment. *Ibid.*; see also Memorandum 19–20.
7. UPS, in a collective-bargaining agreement, had promised to provide temporary alternative work assignments to employees "unable to perform their normal work assignments due to an *on-the-job* injury." App. 547 (emphasis added); see also Memorandum 8, 45–46.
8. The collective-bargaining agreement also provided that UPS would "make a good faith effort to comply . . . with requests for a reasonable accommodation because of a permanent disability" under the ADA. App. 548; see also Memorandum 7.
9. The agreement further stated that UPS would give "inside" jobs to drivers who had lost their DOT certifications because of a failed medical exam, a lost driver's license, or involvement in a motor vehicle accident. See App. 563–565; Memorandum 8.
10. When Young later asked UPS' Capital Division Manager to accommodate her disability, he replied that, while she was pregnant,

she was "too much of a liability" and could "not come back" until she "'was no longer pregnant.'" *Id.,* at 20.

11. Young remained on a leave of absence (without pay) for much of her pregnancy. *Id.,* at 49.
12. Young returned to work as a driver in June 2007, about two months after her baby was born. *Id.,* at 21, 61.

As direct evidence of intentional discrimination, Young relied, in significant part, on the statement of the Capital Division Manager (10 above). As evidence that she had made out a prima facie case under *McDonnell Douglas*, Young relied, in significant part, on evidence showing that UPS would accommodate workers injured on the job (7), those suffering from ADA disabilities (8), and those who had lost their DOT certifications (9). That evidence, she said, showed that UPS had a light-duty-for-injury policy with respect to numerous "other persons," but not with respect to pregnant workers. See Memorandum 29.

Young introduced further evidence indicating that UPS had accommodated several individuals when they suffered disabilities that created work restrictions similar to hers. UPS contests the correctness of some of these facts and the relevance of others. See Brief for Respondent 5, 6, 57. But because we are at the summary judgment stage, and because there is a genuine dispute as to these facts, we view this evidence in the light most favorable to Young, the nonmoving party, see *Scott* v. *Harris*, 550 U. S. 372, 380 (2007):

13. Several employees received accommodations while suffering various similar or more serious disabilities incurred on the job. See App. 400–401 (10– pound lifting limitation); *id.,* at 635 (foot injury); *id.,* at 637 (arm injury).
14. Several employees received accommodations following injury, where the record is unclear as to whether the injury was incurred on or off the job. See *id.,* at 381 (recurring knee injury); *id.,* at 655 (ankle injury); *id.,* at 655 (knee injury); *id.,* at 394−398 (stroke); *id.,* at 425, 636–637 (leg injury).
15. Several employees received "inside" jobs after losing their DOT certifications. See *id.,* at 372 (DOT certification suspended after conviction for driving under the influence); *id.,* at 636, 647 (failed DOT test due to high blood pressure); *id.,* at 640–641 (DOT certification lost due to sleep apnea diagnosis).

16. Some employees were accommodated despite the fact that their disabilities had been incurred off the job. See *id.,* at 446 (ankle injury); *id.,* at 433, 635–636 (cancer).
17. According to a deposition of a UPS shop steward who had worked for UPS for roughly a decade, *id.,* at 461, 463, "the only light duty requested [due to physical] restrictions that became an issue" at UPS "were with women who were pregnant," *id.,* at 504.

The District Court granted UPS' motion for summary judgment. It concluded that Young could not show intentional discrimination through direct evidence. 2011 WL 665321, *10–*12. Nor could she make out a prima facie case of discrimination under *McDonnell Douglas*. The court wrote that those with whom Young compared herself—those falling within the on-the-job, DOT, or ADA categories—were too different to qualify as "similarly situated comparator[s]." 2011 WL 665321, *14. The court added that, in any event, UPS had offered a legitimate, nondiscriminatory reason for failing to accommodate pregnant women, and Young had not created a genuine issue of material fact as to whether that reason was pre-textual. *Id.,* at *15.

On appeal, the Fourth Circuit affirmed. It wrote that "UPS has crafted a pregnancy-blind policy" that is "at least facially a 'neutral and legitimate business practice,' and not evidence of UPS's discriminatory animus toward pregnant workers." 707 F. 3d 437, 446 (2013). It also agreed with the District Court that Young could not show that "similarly-situated employees outside the protected class received more favorable treatment than Young." *Id.*, at 450. Specifically, it believed that Young was different from those workers who were "disabled under the ADA" (which then protected only those with permanent disabilities) because Young was "not disabled"; her lifting limitation was only "temporary and not a significant restriction on her ability to perform major life activities." *Ibid.* Young was also different from those workers who had lost their DOT certifications because "no legal obstacle stands between her and her work" and because many with lost DOT certifications retained physical (*i.e.,* lifting) capacity that Young lacked. *Ibid.* And Young was different from those "injured on the job because, quite simply, her inability to work [did] not arise from an on-the-job injury." *Id.,* at 450–451. Rather, Young more closely resembled "an employee who injured his back while picking up his infant child or . . . an employee whose lifting limitation arose from her off-the-job work as a volunteer firefighter," neither of whom would have been eligible for accommodation under UPS' policies. *Id.,* at 448.

Young filed a petition for certiorari essentially asking us to review the Fourth Circuit's interpretation of the Pregnancy Discrimination Act. In light of lower-court uncertainty about the interpretation of the Act, we granted the petition. Compare *Ensley-Gaines* v. *Runyon*, 100 F. 3d 1220, 1225 (CA6 1996), with *Urbano* v. *Continental Airlines, Inc.*, 138 F. 3d 204, 206–208 (CA5 1998); *Reeves* v. *Swift Transp. Co.*, 446 F. 3d 637, 640–643 (CA6 2006); *Serednyj* v. *Beverly Healthcare, LLC*, 656 F. 3d 540, 547–552 (CA7 2011); *Spivey* v. *Beverly Enterprises, Inc.*, 196 F. 3d 1309, 1312–1314 (CA11 1999).

D

We note that statutory changes made after the time of Young's pregnancy may limit the future significance of our interpretation of the Act. In 2008, Congress expanded the definition of "disability" under the ADA to make clear that "physical or mental impairment[s] that substantially limi[t]" an individual's ability to lift, stand, or bend are ADA-covered disabilities. ADA Amendments Act of 2008, 122 Stat. 3555, codified at 42 U. S. C. §§12102(1)–(2). As interpreted by the EEOC, the new statutory definition requires employers to accommodate employees whose temporary lifting restrictions originate off the job. See 29 CFR pt. 1630, App., §1630.2(j)(1)(ix). We express no view on these statutory and regulatory changes.

II

The parties disagree about the interpretation of the Pregnancy Discrimination Act's second clause. As we have said, see Part I–B, *supra*, the Act's first clause specifies that discrimination " 'because of sex' " includes discrimination "because of . . . pregnancy." But the meaning of the second clause is less clear; it adds: "[W]omen affected by pregnancy, childbirth, or related medical conditions shall be treated the same for all employment-related purposes . . . as *other persons* not so affected but *similar in their ability or inability to work*." 42 U. S. C. §2000e(k) (emphasis added). Does this clause mean that courts must compare workers *only* in respect to the work limitations that they suffer? Does it mean that courts must ignore all other similarities or differences between pregnant and nonpregnant workers? Or does it mean that courts, when deciding who the relevant "other persons" are, may consider other similarities and differences as well? If so, which ones?

The differences between these possible interpretations come to the fore when a court, as here, must consider a workplace policy that distinguishes between pregnant and nonpregnant workers in light of characteristics not related to pregnancy. Young poses the problem directly in her reply brief when she says that the Act requires giving "the same accommodations to an employee with a pregnancy-related work limitation as it would give that employee if her work limitation stemmed from a different cause but had a similar effect on her inability to work." Reply Brief 15. Suppose the employer would not give "that [pregnant] employee" the "same accommodations" as another employee, but the employer's reason for the difference in treatment is that the pregnant worker falls within a facially neutral category (for example, individuals with off-the-job injuries). What is a court then to do?

The parties propose very different answers to this question. Young and the United States believe that the second clause of the Pregnancy Discrimination Act "requires an employer to provide the same accommodations to workplace disabilities caused by pregnancy that it provides to workplace disabilities that have other causes but have a similar effect on the ability to work." Brief for Petitioner 23. In other words, Young contends that the second clause means that whenever "an employer accommodates only a subset of workers with disabling conditions," a court should find a Title VII violation if "pregnant workers who are similar in the ability to work" do not "receive the same [accommodation] even if still other non-pregnant workers do not receive accommodations." *Id.*, at 28.

UPS takes an almost polar opposite view. It contends that the second clause does no more than define sex discrimination to include pregnancy discrimination. See Brief for Respondent 25. Under this view, courts would compare the accommodations an employer provides to pregnant women with the accommodations it provides to others *within* a facially neutral category (such as those with off-the-job injuries) to determine whether the employer has violated Title VII. Cf. *post,* at 4 (SCALIA, J., dissenting) (hereinafter the dissent) (the clause "does not prohibit denying pregnant women accommodations . . . on the basis of an evenhanded policy").

A

We cannot accept either of these interpretations. Young asks us to interpret the second clause broadly and, in her view, literally. As just noted, she argues that, as long as "an employer accommodates only a subset of workers with disabling conditions," "pregnant workers who are similar in the ability to work [must] receive the same treatment even if still other nonpregnant workers do not receive accommodations." Brief for Petitioner 28. She adds that, because the record here contains "evidence that pregnant and nonpregnant workers were not treated the same," that is the end of the matter, she must win; there is no need to refer to *McDonnell Douglas*. Brief for Petitioner 47.

The problem with Young's approach is that it proves too much. It seems to say that the statute grants pregnant workers a "most-favored-nation" status. As long as an employer provides one or two workers with an accommodation—say, those with particularly hazardous jobs, or those whose workplace presence is particularly needed, or those who have worked at the company for many years, or those who are over the age of 55—then it must provide similar accommodations to *all* pregnant workers (with comparable physical limitations), irrespective of the nature of their jobs, the employer's need to keep them working, their ages, or any other criteria.

Lower courts have concluded that this could not have been Congress' intent in passing the Pregnancy Discrimination Act. See, *e.g., Urbano*, 138 F. 3d, at 206–208; *Reeves*, 466 F. 3d, at 641; *Serednyj*, 656 F. 3d, at 548–549; *Spivey*, 196 F. 3d, at 1312–1313. And Young partially agrees, for she writes that "the statute does not require employers to give" to "pregnant workers all of the benefits and privileges it extends to other" similarly disabled "employees when those benefits and privileges are . . . based on the employee's tenure or position within the company." Reply Brief 15–16; see also Tr. of Oral Arg. 22 ("[S]eniority, full-time work, different job classifications, all of those things would be permissible distinctions for an employer to make to differentiate among who gets benefits").

Young's last-mentioned concession works well with respect to seniority, for Title VII itself contains a seniority defense, see 42 U. S. C. §2000e–2(h). Hence, seniority is not part of the problem. But otherwise the most-favored-nation problem remains, and Young's concession does not solve it. How, for example, should a court treat special benefits attached to injuries arising out of, say, extrahazardous duty? If Congress intended to allow differences in treatment arising out of special duties, special service, or special needs, why would it not also have wanted courts to take account of differences arising out of special "causes"—for example, benefits for those who drive (and are injured) in extrahazardous conditions?

We agree with UPS to this extent: We doubt that Congress intended to grant pregnant workers an unconditional most-favored-nation status. The language of the statute does not require that unqualified reading. The second clause, when referring to nonpregnant persons with similar disabilities, uses the open-ended term "other persons." It does not say that the employer must treat pregnant employees the "same" as "*any* other persons" (who are similar in their ability or inability to work), nor does it otherwise specify *which* other persons Congress had in mind.

Moreover, disparate-treatment law normally permits an employer to implement policies that are not intended to harm members of a protected class, even if their implementation sometimes harms those members, as long as the employer has a legitimate, nondiscriminatory, nonpre-textual reason for doing so. See, *e.g., Raytheon*, 540 U. S., at 51–55; *Burdine*, 450 U. S., at 252–258; *McDonnell Douglas*, 411 U. S., at 802. There is no reason to believe Congress intended its language in the Pregnancy Discrimination Act to embody a significant deviation from this approach. Indeed, the relevant House Report specifies that the Act "reflect[s] no new legislative mandate." H. R. Rep. No. 95–948, pp. 3–4 (1978) (hereinafter H. R. Rep.). And the Senate Report states that the Act was designed to "reestablis[h] the law as it was understood prior to" this Court's decision in *General Electric Co.* v. *Gilbert,* 429 U. S. 125 (1976). S. Rep. No. 95–331, p. 8 (1978) (herein-after S. Rep.). See *Gilbert, supra,* at 147 (Brennan, J., dissenting) (lower courts had held that a disability plan that compensates employees for temporary disabilities but not pregnancy violates Title VII); see also *AT&T Corp.* v. *Hulteen*, 556 U. S. 701, 717, n. 2 (2009) (GINSBURG, J., dissenting).

B

Before Congress passed the Pregnancy Discrimination Act, the EEOC issued guidance stating that "[d]isabilities caused or contributed to by pregnancy . . . are, for all job-related purposes, temporary disabilities" and that "the availability of . . . benefits and privileges . . . shall be applied to disability due to pregnancy or childbirth on the same terms and conditions as they are applied to other temporary disabilities." 29 CFR §1604.10(b) (1975). Indeed, as early as 1972, EEOC guidelines provided: "Disabilities caused or contributed to by pregnancy . . . are, for all job-related purposes, temporary disabilities and should be treated as such under any health or temporary disability insurance or sick leave plan available in connection with employment." 37 Fed. Reg. 6837 (1972) (codified in 29 CFR §1604.10(b) (1973)).

Soon after the Act was passed, the EEOC issued guidance consistent with its pre-Act statements. The EEOC explained: "Disabilities caused or contributed to by pregnancy . . . for all job-related purposes, shall be treated the same as disabilities caused or contributed to by other medical conditions." See §1604.10(b) (1979). Moreover, the EEOC stated that "[i]f other employees temporarily unable to lift are relieved of these functions, pregnant employees also unable to lift must be temporarily relieved of the function." 29 CFR pt. 1604, App., p. 918.

This post-Act guidance, however, does not resolve the ambiguity of the term "other persons" in the Act's second clause. Rather, it simply tells employers to treat pregnancyrelated disabilities like nonpregnancy-related disabilities, without clarifying how that instruction should be implemented when an employer does not treat all nonpregnancy-related disabilities alike.

More recently—in July 2014—the EEOC promulgated an additional guideline apparently designed to address this ambiguity. That guideline says that "[a]n employer may not refuse to treat a pregnant worker the same as other employees who are similar in their ability or inability to work by relying on a policy that makes distinctions based on the source of an employee's limitations (e.g., a policy of providing light duty only to workers injured on the job)." 2 EEOC Compliance Manual §626–I(A)(5), p. 626:0009 (July 2014). The EEOC also provided an example of disparate treatment that would violate the Act:

> "An employer has a policy or practice of providing light duty, subject to availability, for any employee who cannot perform one or more job duties for up to 90 days due to injury, illness, or a condition that would be a disability under the ADA. An employee requests a light duty assignment for a 20–pound lift- ing restriction related to her pregnancy. The employer denies the light duty request." *Id.,* at 626:0013, Example 10.

The EEOC further added that "an employer may not deny light duty to a pregnant employee based on a policy that limits light duty to employees with on-the-job injuries." *Id.*, at 626:0028.

The Solicitor General argues that we should give special, if not controlling, weight to this guideline. He points out that we have long held that "the rulings, interpretations and opinions" of an agency charged with the mission of enforcing a particular statute, "while not controlling upon the courts by reason of their authority, do constitute a body of experience and informed judgment to which courts and litigants may properly resort for guidance."

Skidmore v. *Swift & Co.*, 323 U. S. 134, 140 (1944). See Brief for United States as *Amicus Curiae* 26.

But we have also held that the "weight of such a judgment in a particular case will depend upon the thoroughness evident in its consideration, the validity of its reasoning, its consistency with earlier and later pronouncements, and all those factors that give it power to persuade, if lacking power to control." *Skidmore*, *supra*, at 140. These qualifications are relevant here and severely limit the EEOC's July 2014 guidance's special power to persuade.

We come to this conclusion not because of any agency lack of "experience" or "informed judgment." Rather, the difficulties are those of timing, "consistency," and "thoroughness" of "consideration." The EEOC promulgated its 2014 guidelines only recently, after this Court had granted certiorari in this case. In these circumstances, it is fair to say that the EEOC's current guidelines take a position about which the EEOC's previous guidelines were silent. And that position is inconsistent with positions for which the Government has long advocated. See Brief for Defendant-Appellee in *Ensley-Gaines* v. *Runyon*, No. 95–1038 (CA6 1996), pp. 26–27 (explaining that a reading of the Act like Young's was "simply incorrect" and "runs counter" to this Court's precedents). See also Brief for United States as *Amicus Curiae* 16, n. 2 ("The Department of Justice, on behalf of the United States Postal Service, has previously taken the position that pregnant employees with work limitations are not similarly situated to employees with similar limitations caused by on-the-job injuries"). Nor does the EEOC explain the basis of its latest guidance. Does it read the statute, for example, as embodying a most-favored-nation status? Why has it now taken a position contrary to the litigation position the Government previously took? Without further explanation, we cannot rely significantly on the EEOC's determination.

C

We find it similarly difficult to accept the opposite interpretation of the Act's second clause. UPS says that the second clause simply defines sex discrimination to include pregnancy discrimination. See Brief for Respondent 25. But that cannot be so.

The first clause accomplishes that objective when it expressly amends Title VII's definitional provision to make clear that Title VII's words "because of sex" and "on the basis of sex" "include, but are not limited to, because of or on the basis of pregnancy, childbirth, or related medical conditions." 42 U. S. C. §2000e(k). We have long held that " 'a statute ought, upon the whole, to be so construed that, if it can be prevented, no clause' " is rendered " 'superfluous, void, or insignificant.' " *TRW Inc.* v. *Andrews*, 534 U. S. 19, 31 (2001) (quoting *Duncan* v. *Walker*, 533 U. S. 167, 174 (2001)). But that is what UPS' interpretation of the second clause would do.

The dissent, basically accepting UPS' interpretation, says that the second clause is not "superfluous" because it adds "clarity." *Post,* at 4–5 (internal quotation marks omitted). It makes "plain," the dissent adds, that unlawful discrimination "includes disfavoring pregnant women relative to other workers of similar inability to work." *Post,* at 5. Perhaps we fail to understand. *McDonnell Douglas* itself makes clear that courts normally consider how a plaintiff was treated relative to other "persons of [the plaintiff 's] qualifications" (which here include disabilities). 411 U. S., at 802. If the second clause of the Act did not exist, we would still say that an employer who disfavored pregnant women relative to other workers of similar ability or inability to work had engaged in pregnancy discrimination. In a word, there is no need for the "clarification" that the dissent suggests the second sentence provides.

Moreover, the interpretation espoused by UPS and the dissent would fail to carry out an important congressional objective. As we have noted, Congress' "unambiguou[s]" intent in passing the Act was to overturn "both the holding and the reasoning of the Court in the *Gilbert* decision." *Newport News Shipbuilding & Dry Dock Co.* v. *EEOC*, 462 U. S. 669, 678 (1983); see also *post*, at 6 (recognizing that "the object of the Pregnancy Discrimination Act is to displace this Court's conclusion in [*Gilbert*]"). In *Gilbert*, the Court considered a company plan that provided "nonoccupational sickness and accident benefits to all employees" without providing "disability-benefit payments for any absence due to pregnancy." 429 U. S., at 128, 129. The Court held that the plan did not violate Title VII; it did not discriminate on the basis of sex because there was "no risk from which men are protected and women are not." *Id.,* at 138 (internal quotation marks omitted). Although pregnancy is "confined to women," the majority believed it was not "comparable in all other respects to [the] diseases or disabilities" that the plan covered. *Id.,* at 136. Specifically, the majority explained that pregnancy "is not a 'disease' at all," nor is it necessarily a result of accident. *Ibid.* Neither did the majority see the distinction the plan drew as "a subterfuge" or a "pretext" for engaging in gender-based discrimination. *Ibid.* In short, the *Gilbert* majority reasoned in part just as the dissent reasons here. The employer did "not distinguish between pregnant women and others of similar ability or inability *because of pregnancy.*" *Post,* at 2. It distinguished between them on a neutral ground—*i.e.,* it accommodated only sicknesses and accidents, and pregnancy was neither of those. See 429 U. S., at 136.

Simply including pregnancy among Title VII's protected traits (*i.e.,* accepting UPS' interpretation) would not overturn *Gilbert* in full—in particular, it would not respond to *Gilbert*'s determination that an employer can treat pregnancy less favorably than diseases or disabilities resulting in a similar inability to work. As we explained in *California Fed. Sav. & Loan Assn.* v. *Guerra*, 479 U. S. 272 (1987), "the first clause of the [Act] reflects Congress' disapproval of the reasoning in *Gilbert*" by "adding pregnancy to the definition of sex discrimination prohibited by Title VII." *Id.,* at 284. But the second clause was intended to do more than that—it "was intended to overrule the holding in *Gilbert* and to illustrate how discrimination against pregnancy is to be remedied." *Id.,* at 285. The dissent's view, like that of UPS', ignores this precedent.

III

The statute lends itself to an interpretation other than those that the parties advocate and that the dissent sets forth. Our interpretation minimizes the problems we have discussed, responds directly to *Gilbert,* and is consistent with longstanding interpretations of Title VII.

In our view, an individual pregnant worker who seeks to show disparate treatment through indirect evidence maydo so through application of the *McDonnell Douglas* framework. That framework requires a plaintiff to make out a prima facie case of discrimination. But it is "not intended to be an inflexible rule." *Furnco Constr. Corp.* v. *Waters*, 438 U. S. 567, 575 (1978). Rather, an individual plaintiff may establish a prima facie case by "showing actions taken by the employer from which one can infer, if such actions remain unexplained, that it is more likely than not that such actions were based on a discriminatory criterion illegal under" Title VII. *Id.,* at 576 (internal quotation marks omitted). The burden of making this showing is "not onerous." *Burdine*, 450 U. S., at 253. In particular, making this showing is not as burdensome as succeeding on "an ultimate finding of fact as to" a discriminatory employment action. *Furnco*, *supra,* at 576. Neither does it require the plaintiff to show that those whom the employer favored and those whom the employer disfavored were similar in all but the protected ways. See *McDonnell Douglas*, 411 U. S., at 802 (burden met where plaintiff showed that employer hired other "qualified" individuals outside the protected class); *Furnco*, *supra,* at 575–577 (same); *Burdine, supra,* at 253 (same). Cf. *Reeves* v. *Sanderson Plumbing Products, Inc.*, 530 U. S. 133, 142 (2000) (similar).

Thus, a plaintiff alleging that the denial of an accommodation constituted disparate treatment under the Pregnancy Discrimination Act's second clause may make out a prima facie case by showing, as in *McDonnell Douglas*, that she belongs to the protected class, that she sought accommodation, that the employer did not accommodate her, and that the employer did accommodate others "similar in their ability or inability to work."

The employer may then seek to justify its refusal to accommodate the plaintiff by relying on "legitimate, non-discriminatory" reasons for denying her accommodation. 411 U. S., at 802. But, consistent with the Act's basic objective, that reason normally cannot consist simply of a claim that it is more expensive or less convenient to add pregnant women to the category of those ("similar in their ability or inability to work") whom the employer accommodates. After all, the employer in *Gilbert* could in all likelihood have made just such a claim.

If the employer offers an apparently "legitimate, non-discriminatory" reason for its actions, the plaintiff may in turn show that the employer's proffered reasons are in fact pretextual. We believe that the plaintiff may reach a jury on this issue by providing sufficient evidence that the employer's policies impose a significant burden on pregnant workers, and that the employer's "legitimate, nondiscriminatory" reasons are not sufficiently strong to justify the burden, but rather—when considered along with the burden imposed—give rise to an inference of intentional discrimination.

The plaintiff can create a genuine issue of material fact as to whether a significant burden exists by providing evidence that the employer accommodates a large percentage of nonpregnant workers while failing to accommodate a large percentage of pregnant workers. Here, for example, if the facts are as Young says they are, she can show that UPS accommodates most nonpregnant employees with lifting limitations while categorically failing to accommodate pregnant employees with lifting limitations. Young might also add that the fact that UPS has multiple policies that accommodate nonpregnant employees with lifting restrictions suggests that its reasons for failing to accommodate pregnant employees with lifting restrictions are not sufficiently strong—to the point that a jury could find that its reasons for failing to accommodate pregnant employees give rise to an inference of intentional discrimination.

This approach, though limited to the Pregnancy Discrimination Act context, is consistent with our longstanding rule that a plaintiff can use circumstantial proof to rebut an employer's apparently legitimate, nondiscriminatory reasons for treating individuals within a protected class differently than those outside the protected class. See *Burdine*, *supra*, at 255, n. 10. In particular, it is hardly anomalous (as the dissent makes it out to be, see *post*, at 8–9) that a plaintiff may rebut an employer's proffered justifications by showing how a policy operates in practice. In *McDonnell Douglas* itself, we noted that an employer's "general policy and practice with respect to minority employment"—including "statistics as to" that policy and practice—could be evidence of pretext. 411 U. S., at 804–805. Moreover, the continued focus on whether the plaintiff has introduced sufficient evidence to give rise to an inference of *intentional* discrimination avoids confusing the disparate-treatment and disparateimpact doctrines, cf. *post*, at 8–10.

Our interpretation of the Act is also, unlike the dissent's, consistent with Congress' intent to overrule *Gilbert*'s reasoning and result. The dissent says that "[i]f a pregnant woman is denied an accommodation under a policy that does not discriminate against pregnancy, she *has* been 'treated the same' as everyone else." *Post*, at 2. This logic would have found no problem with the employer plan in *Gilbert*, which "denied an accommodation" to pregnant women on the same basis as it denied accommodations to other employees—*i.e.,* it accommodated only sicknesses and accidents, and pregnancy was neither of those. See Part II–C, *supra*. In arguing to the contrary, the dissent's discussion of *Gilbert* relies exclusively on the opinions of the dissenting Justices in that case. See *post*, at 6–7. But Congress' intent in passing the Act was to overrule the *Gilbert majority* opinion, which viewed the employer's disability plan as denying coverage to pregnant employees on a neutral basis.

IV

Under this interpretation of the Act, the judgment of the Fourth Circuit must be vacated. A party is entitled to summary judgment if there is "no genuine dispute as to any material fact and the movant is entitled to judgment as a matter of law." Fed. Rule Civ. Proc. 56(a). We have already outlined the evidence Young introduced. See Part I–C, *supra*. Viewing the record in the light most favorable to Young, there is a genuine dispute as to whether UPS provided more favorable treatment to at least some employees whose situation cannot reasonably be distinguished from Young's. In other words, Young created a genuine dispute of material fact as to the fourth prong of the *McDonnell Douglas* analysis.

Young also introduced evidence that UPS had three separate accommodation policies (on-the-job, ADA, DOT). Taken together, Young argued, these policies significantly burdened pregnant women. See App. 504 (shop steward's testimony that "the only light duty requested [due to physical] restrictions that became an issue" at UPS "were with women who were pregnant"). The Fourth Circuit did not consider the combined effects of these policies, nor did it consider the strength of UPS' justifications for each when combined. That is, why, when the employer accommodated so many, could it not accommodate pregnant women as well?

We do not determine whether Young created a genuine issue of material fact as to whether UPS' reasons for having treated Young less favorably than it treated these other nonpregnant employees were pretextual. We leave a final determination of that question for the Fourth Circuit to make on remand, in light of the interpretation of the Pregnancy Discrimination Act that we have set out above.

* * *

For the reasons above, we vacate the judgment of the Fourth Circuit and remand the case for further proceedings consistent with this opinion.

It is so ordered.

ALITO, J., Concurring in Judgment

SUPREME COURT OF THE UNITED STATES

No. 12–1226

Peggy Young, Petitioner *v.* United Parcel Service, INC.

On Writ of Certiorari to the United States Court of Appeals for the Fourth Circuit

[March 25, 2014]

JUSTICE ALITO, concurring in the judgment.

As originally enacted, Title VII of the Civil Rights Act of 1964, 42 U. S. C. §2000e–2(a)(1), made it an unlawful employment practice to discriminate "because of [an] individual's . . . sex" but made no mention of discrimination because of pregnancy. In *General Elec. Co.* v. *Gilbert*, 429 U. S. 125, 135–140 (1976), this Court held that Title VII did not reach pregnancy discrimination. Congress responded by enacting the Pregnancy Discrimination Act (PDA), which added subsection (k) to a definitional provision, §2000e. Subsection (k) contains two clauses. The first is straightforward; the second is not.

I

The first clause provides that "the terms 'because of sex' or 'on the basis of sex' include, but are not limited to, because of or on the basis of pregnancy."[1] This clause has the effect of adding pregnancy to the list of prohibited grounds (race, sex, etc.) originally included in §2000e–2(a)(1). Claims of discrimination under that provision require proof of discriminatory intent. See, *e.g., Ricci* v. *DeStefano*, 557 U. S. 557, 577 (2009); *Watson* v. *Fort Worth Bank & Trust*, 487 U. S. 977, 985–986 (1988). Thus, as a result of the first clause, an employer engages in unlawful discrimination under §2000e–2(a)(1) if (and only if) the employer's intent is to discriminate because of or on the basis of pregnancy.

If an employer treats a pregnant woman unfavorably for any other reason, the employer is not guilty of an unlawful employment practice under §2000e–2(a), as defined by the first clause of the PDA. And under this first clause, it does not matter whether the employer's ground for the unfavorable treatment is reasonable; all that matters is the employer's actual intent. Of course, when an employer claims to have made a decision for a reason that does not seem to make sense, a factfinder *may* infer that the employer's asserted reason for its action is a pretext for unlawful discrimination. But if the factfinder is convinced that the employer acted for some reason other than pregnancy, the employer cannot be held liable under this clause.

II

The PDA, however, does not simply prohibit discrimination because of or on the basis of pregnancy. Instead, the second clause in §2000e(k) goes on to say the following: "and women affected by pregnancy, childbirth, or related medical conditions shall be treated the same for all employment-related purposes, including receipt of benefits under fringe benefit programs, as other persons not so affected but similar in their ability or inability to work." This clause raises several difficult questions of interpretation that are pertinent to the case now before us.

A

First, does this clause simply explain what is meant by discrimination because of or on the basis of pregnancy? Or does it impose an additional restriction on employer conduct? I believe that this clause does not merely explain but instead adds to the language that precedes it.

This is the interpretation that is most consistent with the statutory text. This clause begins with the word "and," which certainly suggests that what follows represents an addition to what came before.

It is also revealing that the second clause makes no reference to intent, which is the linchpin of liability under the first clause, and that the second clause is an affirmative command (an employer "shall" provide equal treatment), while the first clause is negative (it prohibits discrimination). If a careful drafter wanted to make it clear that the second clause does no more than explain what is meant by the first, the language of the second clause would have to be substantially modified.

Finally, if the second clause does not set out an additional restriction on employer conduct, it would appear to be largely, if not entirely, superfluous. See, *e.g., Arlington Central School Dist. Bd. of Ed.* v. *Murphy*, 548 U. S. 291, 299, n. 1 (2006) ("[I]t is generally presumed that statutes do not contain surplusage"). As noted, the first clause, by adding pregnancy to the list of prohibited grounds for adverse employment actions, mandates that discrimination because of pregnancy be treated like discrimination because of race, sex, etc. An employer commits an unlawful employment practice if it intentionally treats employees of a particular race or sex less favorably than other employees who are similar in their ability or inability to work. Accordingly, the first clause of the PDA is alone sufficient to make it clear that an employer is guilty of an unlawful employment practice if it intentionally treats pregnant employees less favorably than others who are similar in their ability or inability to work.[2] For these reasons, I conclude that the second clause does not merely explain the first but adds a further requirement of equal treatment irrespective of intent.

B

This leads to the second question: In determining whether pregnant employees have been given the equal treatment that this provision demands, with whom must the pregnant employees be compared? I interpret the second clause to mean that pregnant employees must be compared with employees performing the same or very similar jobs. Pregnant employees, the second provision states, must be given the same treatment as other employees who are "similar in their ability or inability to work." An employee's ability to work—despite illness, injury, or pregnancy—often depends on the tasks that the employee's job includes. Different jobs have different tasks, and different tasks require different abilities. Suppose that an employer provides a period of leave with pay for employees whose jobs require tasks, *e.g.*, lifting heavy objects, that they cannot perform because of illness or injury. Must the employer provide the same benefits for pregnant employees who are unable to lift heavy objects but have desk jobs that do not entail heavy lifting? The answer is no. The treatment of pregnant employees must be compared with the treatment of nonpregnant employees whose jobs involve the performance of the same or very similar tasks.

C

This conclusion leads to a third, even more difficult question: When comparing pregnant employees to nonpregnant employees in similar jobs, which characteristics of the pregnant and nonpregnant employees must be taken into account? The answer, I believe, must be found in the reference to "other employees who are similar in their ability or inability to work." I see two possible interpretations of this language. The first is that the capacity to perform the tasks required by a job is the only relevant characteristic, but like the Court, *ante,* at 12–14, I cannot accept this "most favored employee" interpretation.

This interpretation founders when, as in this case, an employer treats pregnant women less favorably than some but not all nonpregnant employees who have similar jobs and are similarly impaired in their ability to perform the tasks that these jobs require. In this case, as I will explain below, see Part III, United Parcel Service (UPS) drivers who were unable to perform the physical tasks required by that job fell into three groups: first, nonpregnant employees who received favorable treatment; second, nonpregnant employees who do not receive favorable treatment; and third, pregnant employees who, like the nonpregnant employees in the second category, did not receive favorable treatment. Under these circumstances, would the "most favored employee" interpretation require the employer to treat the pregnant women like the employees in the first, favored group? Or would it be sufficient if the employer treated them the same as the non-pregnant employees in the second group who did not receive favorable treatment?

Recall that the second clause of §2000e(k) requires that pregnant women "be treated the same for all employment-related purposes . . . as *other persons* not so affected but similar in their ability or inability to work." (Emphasis added.) Therefore, UPS could say that its policy treated the pregnant employees the same as "other persons" who were similar in their ability or inability to work, namely, those nonpregnant employees in the second category. But at the same time, the pregnant drivers like petitioner could say that UPS did not treat them the same as "other employees" who were similar in their ability or inability to work, namely, the nonpregnant employees in the first group. An interpretation that leads to such a problem cannot be correct.[3]

I therefore turn to the other possible interpretation of the phrase "similar in their ability or inability to work," namely, that "similar in the ability or inability to work" means "similar *in relation* to the ability or inability to work."[4] Under this interpretation, pregnant and non-pregnant employees are not similar in relation to the ability or inability to work if they are unable to work for different reasons. And this means that these two groups of employees are not similar in the relevant sense if the employer has a neutral business reason for treating them differently. I agree with the Court that a sufficient reason "normally cannot consist simply of a claim that it is more expensive or less convenient to add pregnant women to the category of those . . . whom the employer accommodates." *Ante*, at 21.[5] Otherwise, however, I do not think that the second clause of the PDA authorizes courts to evaluate the justification for a truly neutral rule. The language used in the second clause of the PDA is quite different from that used in other antidiscrimination provisions that require such an evaluation. Cf. §12112(b)(5)(A) (discrimination against a person with a disability includes "not making *reasonable accommodations* to the known physical or mental limitations of an otherwise qualified . . . employee, unless [the employer] can demonstrate that the accommodation would impose *an undue hardship* on the operation of [its] business" (emphasis added)); §2000e(j) (employer must reasonably accommodate religious observance, practice, and belief unless that would impose an "undue hardship on the conduct of the employer's business"); §2000e–2(k)(1)(A)(i) (business necessity defense in Title VII disparate-impact cases).

III

I understand petitioner in this case to assert claims under both the first and second clauses of §2000e(k). With respect to her claim under the first clause, I agree with the Court that the information in the summary judgment record is sufficient (albeit barely) to take the question to the trier of fact.

I believe that the judgment of the Court of Appeals with respect to petitioner's claim under the second clause must also be vacated. Petitioner sought to be excused during her pregnancy from the lifting requirements that were among her tasks as a driver. Under the policy that United Parcel Service claims to have had in force at the time in question, drivers who were physically unable to perform the tasks required by that position fell into three groups.

First, some drivers were reassigned to less physically demanding positions. Included in this group were (a) those who were unable to work as drivers due to an injury incurred on the job, (b) those drivers who were unable to work as drivers due to a disability as defined by the Americans With Disabilities Act of 1990 (ADA), and (c) those drivers who, as the result of a medical condition or injury, lost the Department of Transportation (DOT) certification needed to work in that capacity.

The second group of drivers consisted of those who were not pregnant and were denied transfer to a light-duty job. Drivers who were injured off the job fell into this category. The third group was made up of pregnant drivers like petitioner.

It is obvious that respondent had a neutral reason for providing an accommodation when that was required by the ADA. Respondent also had neutral grounds for providing special accommodations for employees who were injured on the job. If these employees had not been permitted to work at all, it appears that they would have been eligible for workers' compensation benefits. See Md. Lab. & Empl. Code Ann. §9–614 (2008).

The accommodations that are provided to drivers who lost their DOT certifications, however, are another matter. A driver may lose DOT certification for a variety of reasons, including medical conditions or injuries incurred off the job that impair the driver's ability to operate a motor vehicle. Such drivers may then be transferred to jobs that do not require physical tasks incompatible with their illness or injury. It does not appear that respondent has provided any plausible justification for treating these drivers more favorably than drivers who were pregnant.

The Court of Appeals provided two grounds for distinguishing petitioner's situation from that of the drivers who had lost their DOT certifications, see 707 F. 3d 437, 450 (CA4 2013), but neither is adequate. First, the Court of Appeals noted that "no legal obstacle [stood] between [petitioner] and her work." *Ibid.* But the legal obstacle faced by drivers who have lost DOT certification only explains why those drivers could not continue to perform all the tasks required by their ordinary jobs; it does not explain why respondent went further and *provided such drivers with a work accommodation.* Petitioner's pregnancy prevented her from continuing her normal work as a driver, just as is the case for a driver who loses DOT certification. But respondent had a policy of accommodating drivers who lost DOT certification but not accommodating pregnant women, like petitioner. The legal obstacle of lost certification cannot explain this difference in treatment.

Second, the Court of Appeals observed that "'those with DOT certification maintai[n] the ability to perform any number of demanding physical tasks,'" *ibid.*, but it is doubtful that this is true in all instances. A driver can lose DOT certification due to a great variety of medical conditions, including loss of a limb, 49 CFR §391.41(b)(1) (2013); impairments of the arm, hand, finger, foot, or leg, §391.41(b)(2)(i) and (ii); cardiovascular disease, §391.41(b)(4); respiratory dysfunction, §391.41(b)(5); high blood pressure, §391.41(b)(6); arthritis, §391.41(b)(7); and epilepsy §391.41(b)(8). It is not evident—and as far as I am aware, the record does not show—that all drivers with these conditions are nevertheless able to perform a great many physically demanding tasks. Nevertheless, respondent says that it was its policy to transfer such drivers to so-called inside jobs when such positions were available. Presumably, respondent did not assign these drivers to jobs that they were physically unable to perform. So in at least some instances, they must have been assigned to jobs that did not require them to perform tasks that they were incapable of performing due to the medical condition that caused the loss of DOT certification. Respondent has not explained why pregnant drivers could not have been given similar consideration.

For these reasons, it is not at all clear that respondent had any neutral business ground for treating pregnant drivers less favorably than at least some of its nonpregnant drivers who were reassigned to other jobs that they were physically capable of performing. I therefore agree with the Court that the decision of the Court of Appeals with respect to petitioner's claim under the second clause of the PDA must be vacated, and the case must be re-manded for further proceedings with respect to that claim.

SCALIA, J., dissenting

SUPREME COURT OF THE UNITED STATES

No. 12–1226

Peggy Young, Petitioner v. United Parcel Service, INC.

On Writ of Certiorari to the United States court of Appeals for the Fourth Circuit

[March 25, 2015]

JUSTICE SCALIA, with whom JUSTICE KENNEDY and JUSTICE THOMAS join, dissenting.

Faced with two conceivable readings of the Pregnancy Discrimination Act, the Court chooses neither. It crafts instead a new law that is splendidly unconnected with the text and even the legislative history of the Act. To "treat" pregnant workers "the same . . . as other persons," we are told, means refraining from adopting policies that impose "significant burden[s]" upon pregnant women without "sufficiently strong" justifications. *Ante,* at 21. Where do the "significant burden" and "sufficiently strong justification" requirements come from? Inventiveness posing as scholarship—which gives us an interpretation that is as dubious in principle as it is senseless in practice.

I

Title VII forbids employers to discriminate against employees "because of . . . sex." 42 U. S. C. §2000e–2(a)(1). The Pregnancy Discrimination Act adds a provision to Title VII's definitions section:

> "The terms 'because of sex' or 'on the basis of sex' in- clude, but are not limited to, because of or on the basis of pregnancy, childbirth, or related medical condi- tions; and women affected by pregnancy, childbirth, or related medical conditions shall be treated the same for all employment-related purposes, including receipt of benefits under fringe benefit programs, as other persons not so affected but similar in their ability or inability to work . . . ." §2000e(k).

Title VII's prohibition of discrimination creates liability for both disparate treatment (taking action with "discriminatory motive") and disparate impact (using a practice that "fall[s] more harshly on one group than another and cannot be justified by business necessity"). *Teamsters* v. *United States*, 431 U. S. 324, 335–336, n. 15 (1977). Peggy Young did not establish pregnancy discrimination under either theory. She argued that United Parcel Service's refusal to accommodate her inability to work amounted to disparate treatment, but the Court of Appeals concluded that she had not mustered evidence that UPS denied the accommodation with intent to disfavor pregnant women. 707 F. 3d 437, 449–451 (CA4 2013). And Young never brought a claim of disparate impact.

That is why Young and the Court leave behind the part of the law defining pregnancy discrimination as sex discrimination, and turn to the part requiring that "women affected by pregnancy . . . be treated the same . . . as other persons not so affected but similar in their ability or inability to work." §2000e(k). The most natural way to understand the same-treatment clause is that an employer may not distinguish between pregnant women and others of similar ability or inability *because of pregnancy*. Here, that means pregnant women are entitled to accommodations *on the same terms* as other workers with disabling conditions. If a pregnant woman is denied an accommodation under a policy that does not discriminate against pregnancy, she *has* been "treated the same" as everyone else. UPS's accommodation for drivers who lose their certifications illustrates the point. A pregnant woman who loses her certification gets the benefit, just like any other worker who loses his. And a pregnant woman who keeps her certification does not get the benefit, again just like any other worker who keeps his. That certainly sounds like treating pregnant women and others the same.

There is, however, another way to understand "treated the same," at least looking at that phrase on its own. One could read it to mean that an employer may not distinguish *at all* between pregnant women and others of similar ability. Here, that would mean pregnant women are entitled, not to accommodations on the same terms as others, but to *the same accommodations* as others, no matter the differences (other than pregnancy) between them. UPS's accommodation for decertified drivers illustrates this usage too. There is a sense in which a pregnant woman denied an accommodation (because she kept her certification) has *not* been treated the same as an injured man granted an accommodation (because he lost his certification). He got the accommodation and she did not.

Of these two readings, only the first makes sense in the context of Title VII. The point of Title VII's bans on discrimination is to prohibit employers from treating one worker differently from another *because of a protected trait*. It is not to prohibit employers from treating workers differently for reasons that have nothing to do with protected traits. See *Texas Dept. of Community Affairs* v. *Burdine*, 450 U. S. 248, 259 (1981). Against that back-drop, a requirement that pregnant women and other workers be treated the same is sensibly read to forbid distinctions that discriminate against pregnancy, not all distinctions whatsoever.

Prohibiting employers from making *any* distinctions between pregnant workers and others of similar ability would elevate pregnant workers to most favored employees. If Boeing offered chauffeurs to injured directors, it would have to offer chauffeurs to pregnant mechanics. And if Disney paid pensions to workers who can no longer work because of old age, it would have to pay pensions to workers who can no longer work because of childbirth. It is implausible that Title VII, which elsewhere creates guarantees of *equal* treatment, here alone creates a guarantee of *favored* treatment.

Let it not be overlooked, moreover, that the thrust of the Pregnancy Discrimination Act is that pregnancy discrimination is sex discrimination. Instead of creating a freestanding ban on pregnancy discrimination, the Act makes plain that the existing ban on sex discrimination reaches discrimination because of pregnancy. Reading the same-treatment clause to give pregnant women special protection unavailable to other women would clash with this central theme of the Act, because it would mean that pregnancy discrimination differs from sex discrimination after all.

All things considered, then, the right reading of the same-treatment clause prohibits practices that discriminate against pregnant women relative to workers of similar ability or inability. It does not prohibit denying pregnant women accommodations, or any other benefit for that matter, on the basis of an evenhanded policy.

II

The Court agrees that the same-treatment clause is not a most-favored-employee law, *ante*, at 12, but at the same time refuses to adopt the reading I propose—which is the only other reading the clause could conceivably bear. The Court's reasons for resisting this reading fail to persuade.

The Court starts by arguing that the same-treatment clause must do more than ban distinctions on the basis of pregnancy, lest it add nothing to the part of the Act defining pregnancy discrimination as sex discrimination. *Ante*, at 17. Even so read, however, the same-treatment clause *does* add something: clarity. See *Newport News Ship-building & Dry Dock Co.* v. *EEOC*, 462 U. S. 669, 678, n. 14 (1983) ("[T]he specific language in the second clause . . . explains the application of the [first clause]"). Just defining pregnancy discrimination as sex discrimination does not tell us what it means to discriminate because of pregnancy. Does pregnancy discrimination include, in addition to disfavoring pregnant women relative to the workplace in general, disfavoring them relative to disabled workers in particular? Concretely, does an employer engage in pregnancy discrimination by excluding pregnancy from an otherwise complete disability-benefits program? Without the same-treatment clause, the answers to these questions would not be obvious. An employer could argue that people do not necessarily think of pregnancy and childbirth as disabilities. Or that it would be anomalous to read a law defining pregnancy discrimination as sex discrimination to require him to treat *pregnancy* like a disability, when Title VII does not require him to treat *sex* like a disability. Or that even if pregnancy were a disability, it would be *sui generis*—categorically different from all other disabling conditions. Cf. *Geduldig* v. *Aiello*, 417 U. S. 484, 494–495 (1974) (holding that a State has a rational basis for excluding pregnancy-related disabilities from a disability-benefits program). With the sametreatment clause, these doubts disappear. By requiring that women affected by pregnancy "be treated the same . . . *as other persons not so affected but similar in their ability or inability to work*" (emphasis added), the clause makes plain that pregnancy discrimination includes disfavoring pregnant women relative to other workers of similar inability to work.

This clarifying function easily overcomes any charge that the reading I propose makes the same-treatment clause " 'superfluous, void, or insignificant.' " *Ante,* at 17–18. Perhaps, as the Court suggests, even without the same-treatment clause the best reading of the Act would prohibit disfavoring pregnant women relative to disabled workers. But laws often make explicit what might already have been implicit, "for greater caution" and in order "to leave nothing to construction." The Federalist No. 33, pp. 205–206 (J. Cooke ed. 1961) (A. Hamilton). That is why we have long acknowledged that a "sufficient" explanation for the inclusion of a clause can be "found in the desire to remove all doubts" about the meaning of the rest of the text. *McCulloch* v. *Maryland*, 4 Wheat. 316, 420 (1819). This explanation looks all the more sensible once one remembers that the object of the Pregnancy Discrimination Act is to displace this Court's conclusion in *General Elec. Co.* v. *Gilbert*, 429 U. S. 125 (1976), that pregnancy discrimination is not sex discrimination. What could be more natural than for a law whose object is superseding earlier judicial interpretation to include a clause whose object is leaving nothing to future judicial interpretation?

That brings me to the Court's remaining argument: the claim that the reading I have set forth would not suffice to overturn our decision in *Gilbert*. *Ante,* at 18–20. Wrong. *Gilbert* upheld an otherwise comprehensive disability-benefits plan that singled pregnancy out for disfavor. The most natural reading of the Act overturns that decision, because it prohibits singling pregnancy out for disfavor.

The Court goes astray here because it mistakenly assumes that the *Gilbert* plan excluded pregnancy on "a neutral ground"—covering sicknesses and accidents but nothing else. *Ante,* at 19. In reality, the plan in *Gilbert* was not neutral toward pregnancy. It "place[d] . . . pregnancy in a class by itself," treating it differently from "any other kind" of condition. 429 U. S., at 161 (Stevens, J., dissenting). At the same time that it denied coverage for pregnancy, it provided coverage for a comprehensive range of other conditions, including many that one would not necessarily call sicknesses or accidents—like "sport injuries, attempted suicides, . . . disabilities incurred in the commission of a crime or during a fight, and elective cosmetic surgery," *id.,* at 151 (Brennan, J., dissenting). What is more, the plan denied coverage even to sicknesses, if they were related to pregnancy or childbirth. *Ibid.* For that matter, the plan denied coverage to sicknesses that were *unrelated* to pregnancy or childbirth, if they were suffered during recovery from the birth of a child. *Ibid. Gilbert*, there can be no doubt, involved "the lone exclusion of pregnancy from [a] program." *Ibid.* The most natural interpretation of the Act easily suffices to make that unlawful.

III

Dissatisfied with the only two readings that the words of the same-treatment clause could possibly bear, the Court decides that the clause means something in-between. It takes only a couple of waves of the Supreme Wand to produce the desired result. Poof!: The same-treatment clause means that a neutral reason for refusing to accommodate a pregnant woman is pretextual if "the employer's policies impose a significant burden on pregnant workers." *Ante,* at 21. Poof!: This is so only when the employer's reasons "are not sufficiently strong to justify the burden." *Ibid.*

How we got here from the same-treatment clause is anyone's guess. There is no way to read "shall be treated the same"—or indeed anything else in the clause—to mean that courts must balance the significance of the burden on pregnant workers against the strength of the employer's justifications for the policy. That is presumably why the Court does not even *try* to connect the interpretation it adopts with the text it purports to interpret. The Court has forgotten that statutory purpose and the presumption against superfluity are tools for choosing among competing reasonable readings of a law, not authorizations for making up new readings that the law cannot reasonably bear.

The fun does not stop there. Having ignored the terms of the same-treatment clause, the Court proceeds to bungle the dichotomy between claims of disparate treatment and claims of disparate impact. Normally, liability for disparate treatment arises when an employment policy has a "discriminatory motive," while liability for disparate impact arises when the effects of an employment policy "fall more harshly on one group than another and cannot be justified by business necessity." *Teamsters*, 431 U. S., at 336, n. 15. In the topsyturvy world created by today's decision, however, a pregnant woman can establish disparate *treatment* by showing that the effects of her employer's policy fall more harshly on pregnant women than on others (the policies "impose a significant burden on pregnant workers," *ante,* at 21) and are inadequately justified (the "reasons are not sufficiently strong to justify the burden," *ibid.*). The change in labels may be small, but the change in results assuredly is not. Disparate-treatment and disparate-impact claims come with different standards of liability, different defenses, and different remedies. *E.g.*, 42 U. S. C. §§1981a, 2000e–2(k). For example, plaintiffs in disparate-treatment cases can get compensatory and punitive damages as well as equitable relief, but plaintiffs in disparate impact cases can get equitable relief only. See §§1981a, 2000e–5(g). A sound reading of the same-treatment clause would preserve the distinctions so carefully made elsewhere in the Act; the Court's reading makes a muddle of them.

But (believe it or not) it gets worse. In order to make sense of its conflation of disparate impact with disparate treatment, the Court claims that its new test is somehow "limited to the Pregnancy Discrimination Act context," yet at the same time "consistent with" the traditional use of circumstantial evidence to show intent to discriminate in Title VII cases. *Ante,* at 22. A court in a Title VII case, true enough, may consider a policy's effects and even its justifications—along with " 'all of the [other] surrounding facts and circumstances' "—when trying to ferret out a policy's motive. *Hazelwood School Dist.* v. *United States*, 433 U. S. 299, 312 (1977). The Court cannot possibly think, however, that its newfangled balancing test reflects this conventional inquiry. It has, after all, just marched up and down the hill telling us that the same-treatment clause is not (no-no!) " 'superfluous, void, or insignificant.'" *Ante,* at 17–18. If the clause merely instructed courts to consider a policy's effects and justifications the way it considers other circumstantial evidence of motive, it *would* be superfluous. So the Court's balancing test must mean something else. Even if the effects and justifications of policies are not enough to show intent to discriminate under ordinary Title VII principles, they could (Poof !) still show intent to discriminate for purposes of the pregnancy same-treatment clause. Deliciously incoherent.

And all of this to what end? The difference between a routine circumstantial-evidence inquiry into motive and today's grotesque effects-and-justifications inquiry into motive, it would seem, is that today's approach requires judges to concentrate on effects and justifications to the exclusion of other considerations. But Title VII *already* has a framework that allows judges to home in on a policy's effects and justifications—disparate impact. Under that framework, it is *already* unlawful for an employer to use a practice that has a disparate impact on the basis of a protected trait, unless (among other things) the employer can show that the practice "is job related . . . and consistent with business necessity." §2000e–2(k)(1)(A)(i). The Court does not explain why we need (never mind how the Act could possibly be read to contain) today's ersatz disparate-impact test, under which the disparate-impact element gives way to the significant-burden criterion and the business-necessity defense gives way to the sufficiently-strong-justification standard. Today's decision can thus serve only one purpose: allowing claims that belong under Title VII's disparate-impact provisions to be brought under its disparate-treatment provisions instead.

IV

JUSTICE ALITO'S concurrence agrees with the Court's rejection of both conceivable readings of the same-treatment clause, but fashions a different compromise between them. Under its approach, an employer may deny a pregnant woman a benefit granted to workers who perform similar tasks only on the basis of a "neutral business ground." *Ante,* at 10 (opinion concurring in judgment). This requirement of a "business ground" shadows the Court's requirement of a "sufficiently strong" justification, and, like it, has no footing in the terms of the same-treatment clause. As the concurrence understands the words "shall be treated the same," an employer must give pregnant workers the same accommodations (not merely accommodations on the same terms) as other workers "who are similar in their ability or inability to work." *Ante,* at 3–4. But the concurrence realizes that requiring the same accommodations to all who are similar in ability or inability to work—the only characteristic mentioned in the same-treatment clause—would "lead to wildly implausible results." *Ante,* at 6, n. 3. To solve this problem, the concurrence broadens the category of characteristics that the employer may take into account. It allows an employer to find dissimilarity on the basis of traits *other* than ability to work so long as there is a "neutral business reason" for considering them—though it immediately adds that cost and inconvenience are not good enough reasons. *Ante,* at 7. The need to engage in this text-free broadening in order to make the concurrence's interpretation work is as good a sign as any that its interpretation is wrong from the start.

* * *

My disagreement with the Court is fundamental. I think our task is to choose the best possible reading of the law—that is, what text and context most strongly suggest it conveys. The Court seems to think our task is to craft a policy-driven compromise between the possible readings of the law, like a congressional conference committee reconciling House and Senate versions of a bill.

Because Young has not established that UPS's accommodations policy discriminates against pregnant women relative to others of similar ability or inability, see *supra,* at 2, she has not shown a violation of the Act's same-treatment requirement. I would therefore affirm the judgment of the Court of Appeals for the Fourth Circuit.

KENNEDY, J., Dissenting

SUPREME COURT OF THE UNITED STATES

No. 12–1226

Peggy Young, Petitioner v. United Parcel Service, INC.

On Writ of Certiorari to the United States Court of Appeals for the Fourth Circuit

[March 25, 2015]

JUSTICE KENNEDY, dissenting.

It seems to me proper, in joining JUSTICE SCALIA's dissent, to add these additional remarks. The dissent is altogether correct to point out that petitioner here cannot point to a class of her co-workers that was accommodated and that would include her but for the particular limitations imposed by her pregnancy. Many other workers with health-related restrictions were not accommodated either. And, in addition, there is no showing here of animus or hostility to pregnant women.

But as a matter of societal concern, indifference is quite another matter. There must be little doubt that women who are in the work force—by choice, by financial necessity, or both—confront a serious disadvantage after becoming pregnant. They may find it difficult to continue to work, at least in their regular assignment, while still taking necessary steps to avoid risks to their health and the health of their future children. This is why the difficulties pregnant women face in the workplace are and do remain an issue of national importance.

"Historically, denial or curtailment of women's employment opportunities has been traceable directly to the pervasive presumption that women are mothers first, and workers second." *Nevada Dept. of Human Resources* v. *Hibbs*, 538 U. S. 721, 736 (2003) (quoting The Parental and Medical Leave Act of 1986: Joint Hearing before the Subcommittee on Labor–Management Relations and the Subcommittee on Labor Standards of the House Committee on Education and Labor, 99th Cong., 2d Sess., 100 (1986)). Such "attitudes about pregnancy and childbirth . . . have sustained pervasive, often law-sanctioned, restrictions on a woman's place among paid workers." *AT&T*

Corp. v. *Hulteen*, 556 U. S. 701, 724 (2009) (GINSBURG, J., dissenting). Although much progress has been made in recent decades and many employers have voluntarily adopted policies designed to recruit, accommodate, and retain employees who are pregnant or have young children, see Brief for U. S. Women's Chamber of Commerce et al., as *Amici Curiae* 10–14, pregnant employees continue to be disadvantaged—and often discriminated against—in the workplace, see Brief of Law Professors et al., as *Amici Curiae* 37–38.

Recognizing the financial and dignitary harm caused by these conditions, Congress and the States have enacted laws to combat or alleviate, at least to some extent, the difficulties faced by pregnant women in the work force. Most relevant here, Congress enacted the Pregnancy Discrimination Act (PDA), 42 U. S. C. §2000e(k), which defines discrimination on the basis of pregnancy as sex discrimination for purposes of Title VII and clarifies that pregnant employees "shall be treated the same" as nonpregnant employees who are "similar in their ability or inability to work." The PDA forbids not only disparate treatment but also disparate impact, the latter of which prohibits "practices that are not intended to discriminate but in fact have a disproportionate adverse effect." *Ricci* v. *DeStefano*, 557 U. S. 557, 577 (2009). Congress further enacted the parental-leave provision of the Family and Medical Leave Act of 1993, 29 U. S. C. §2612(a)(1)(A), which requires certain employers to provide eligible employees with 12 workweeks of leave because of the birth of a child. And after the events giving rise to this litigation, Congress passed the ADA Amendments Act of 2008, 122 Stat. 3553, which expands protections for employees with temporary disabilities. As the parties note, Brief for Petitioner 37–43; Brief for Respondent 21–22; Brief for United States as *Amicus Curiae* 24–25, these amendments and their implementing regulations, 29 CFR §1630 (2015), may require accommodations for many pregnant employees, even though pregnancy itself is not expressly classified as a disability. Additionally, many States have enacted laws providing certain accommodations for pregnant employees. See, *e.g.*, Cal. Govt. Code Ann. §12945 (West 2011); La. Rev. Stat. Ann. §23:342(4) (West 2010); W. Va. Code Ann. §5–11B–2 (Lexis Supp. 2014); see also *California Fed. Sav. & Loan Assn.* v. *Guerra*, 479 U. S. 272 (1987) (holding that the PDA does not pre-empt such statutes). These Acts honor and safeguard the important contributions women make to both the workplace and the American family.

Today the Court addresses only one of these legal protections: the PDA's prohibition of disparate treatment. For the reasons well stated in JUSTICE

SCALIA's dissenting opinion, the Court interprets the PDA in a manner that risks "conflation of disparate impact with disparate treatment" by permitting a plaintiff to use a policy's disproportionate burden on pregnant employees as evidence of pretext. *Ante,* at 8; see *ante,* at 21–22 (opinion of the Court). In so doing, the Court injects unnecessary confusion into the accepted burden-shifting framework established in *McDonnell Douglas Corp.* v. *Green*, 411 U. S. 792 (1973).

With these remarks, I join JUSTICE SCALIA'S dissent.

End Notes

[1] While §2000e–2(a) uses the phrase "because of . . . sex," other provi- sions governed by the definitions in §2000e use the phrase "on the basis of . . . sex." See, *e.g.*, §§2000e–2(b), (k)(1)(A). Therefore, subsection (k) covers this phrase as well.

[2] JUSTICE SCALIA's dissent argues, *post,* at 4–6, that the second clause serves the useful purpose of clarifying the meaning of discrimination because of pregnancy. Without the second clause, that dissent main- tains, there might be uncertainty as to whether an employer would commit an unlawful employment practice if it excluded pregnancy from an otherwise complete disability benefits program. Contrary to the dissent, however, I think that the answer to this question would be quite obvious based on the first clause of the PDA alone. If an employer provided benefits for every employee who was temporarily unable to work due to any physical condition other than pregnancy, that em- ployer would be in the same position as an employer who provided similar benefits for employees of every race but one. In both situations, the employer would clearly discriminate on a prohibited ground.

[3] The "most favored employee" interpretation would also lead to wildly implausible results. Suppose, for example, that an employer had a policy of refusing to provide any accommodation for any employee who was unable to work due to any reason but that the employer wished to make an exception for several employees who were seriously injured while performing acts of extraordinary heroism on the job, for example, saving the lives of numerous fellow employees during a fire in the workplace. If the ability to perform job tasks was the only characteris- tic that could be considered, the employer would face the choice of either denying any special treatment for the heroic employees or providing all the same benefits to all pregnant employees. It is most unlikely that this is what Congress intended. Such a requirement would go beyond anything demanded by any other antidiscrimination law.

[4] Opinions have often used the phrase "similar in" to mean "similar in relation to" or "similar with respect to." See, *e.g., Kiobel* v. *Royal Dutch Petroleum Co*., 569 U. S. , (2013) (BREYER, J., concurring in judgment) (slip op., at 3) ("similar in character and specificity to piracy"); *Williams* v. *Illinois*, 567 U. S. , (2012) (THOMAS, J., concur- ring in judgment) (slip op., at 10) ("similar in solemnity to the Marian examination practices that the Confrontation Clause was designed to prevent"). *Sykes* v. *United States*, 564 U. S. , (2011) (slip op., at 6) ("similar in degree of danger to that involved in arson").

[5] If cost alone could justify unequal treatment of pregnant employees, the plan at issue in *General Electric Co.* v. *Gilbert*, 429 U. S. 125 (1976), would be lawful. Cf. *id.*, at 138. But this Court has repeatedly said that the PDA rejected " 'both the holding and the reasoning' " in *Gilbert*. *AT&T* v. *Hulteen*, 556 U. S. 701, 720 (2009) (GINSBURG, J., dissenting) (quoting *Newport News Shipbuilding & Dry Dock Co.* v. *EEOC*, 462 U. S. 669, 678 (1983).

INDEX

A

B

C

D

E

F

G

H

S

T

U

V

W

Y